workspaces

TEXT
martha fay

PHOTOGRAPHY
mark lund

STYLING
michael walters

EXECUTIVE EDITOR
clay ide

BONNIER
BOOKS

This edition published by Bonnier Books,
Appledram Barns, Birdham Road, Chichester,
West Sussex PO20 7EQ, UK

WELDON OWEN

Chief Executive Officer John Owen
President & Chief Operating Officer Terry Newell
Chief Financial Officer Christine E. Munson
Vice President, Creative Director Gaye Allen
Vice President, Publisher Roger Shaw
Vice President, International Sales Stuart Laurence

Associate Publisher Shawna Mullen
Art Director Colin Wheatland
Managing Editor Sarah Lynch
Production Director Chris Hemesath
Colour Manager Teri Bell
Photo Co-ordinator Elizabeth Lazich
UK Translation Grant Laing Partnership

Set in Simoncini Garamond™ and Formata™

Colour separations by International Color Services
Printed in Singapore by Tien Wah Press (Pte.) Ltd.

Originally published as *Pottery Barn Workspaces* in 2004.
10 9 8 7 6 5 4 3 2 1

ISBN: 978-1-905825-06-6

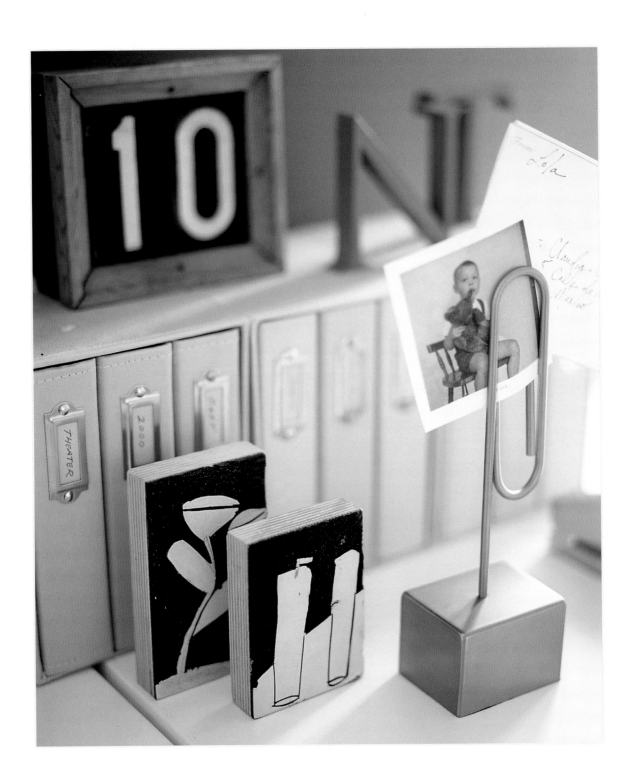

Working with Style

A comfortable reading chair, the perfect desk lamp, a wall of favourite photos. Working at home has an appeal that's hard to match. Whether it's in a traditional home office, an artist's studio, or a kitchen corner, the perfect workspace is one that works just the way you do. We all want our home offices to be stylish and functional, to hold a bit of the past but offer the conveniences of the present. The best workspaces do this and more – they are retreats that inspire the imagination, settings that reflect personality, and rooms that help focus attention on the task at hand.

A truly great workspace balances organization with comfort and style. This book is designed to assist you along the way, and to help you create a work area that has your own special touch. Each chapter offers a wealth of ideas and options to choose from, whether your work includes books and files, garden projects, or managing a busy household. We've photographed all the images in this book in real homes, and we offer easy ways to apply the ideas you see in these pages to your own workspace. The information presented here can be readily adapted to rooms of all different shapes, sizes, and uses. In *Workspaces*, you'll find the essential tools, practical wisdom, and creative encouragement you need to make your space a wonderful place to work.

contents

monday   tuesday   wednesday

THANK YOU

+DUPLEX
7:15 PM Sun 09/28/03
AD PRI $9.00
Kabuki 8

Customer Copy

your style

The very term *workspace* conjures different images for each of us. To some, it evokes an abundance of shiny tools neatly arranged on a sturdy worktable. For others, it's a small, uncluttered space with only a chair, a desk, and a favourite lamp to write by or a clear wash of northern light to paint by. Whether it's a professional home office, a corner of the living room, or reclaimed space in an attic, a workroom comes closest to satisfying the longing for the elusive "room of one's own" – and offers an irresistible opportunity to create one.

Other things to consider are those more specific to the type of work you do and the furnishings that make the most sense for it: a desk for a home office or a large table for an artist's studio. Choosing the right kind of storage – open or closed, free-standing or built-in – and a sufficient combination of types of lighting takes careful planning, too. Keep in mind office ergonomics as well: table height, chair comfort, room to stretch, and ventilation. Is there space for a chaise longue or an exercise mat? Shared workspaces pose special challenges but frequently yield design

The ideal workspace marries purpose and passion. Design your home office to inspire creativity, to offer delight, and to help you complete the job at hand.

As a matter of personal taste, a workspace can be elegant or rustic, sleek or cosy, traditional or individual. As a practical matter, what you're aiming for is ease of use and a place you look forward to returning to day after day. Think about what makes you happiest when you work. Is it an inspiring view, or an absence of clutter? Some of us work best when everything is within easy reach; others enjoy having an excuse to cross the room for a fresh stack of printer paper. Perhaps you'd like to have a cosy chair for reading or a day-bed for quick catnaps. Maybe you crave extra privacy; conversely, perhaps you'd prefer a large desk that you can share with your spouse.

bonuses. Placing desks back to back or finding other methods of creative zoning will allow a space to serve more than one user at a time.

If space is tight, carve a workroom or home office from an open stairwell or an attic dormer. Make it your own by adding personal touches to its utilitarian bones: a splash of colour on a back wall, a gallery of drawings or family photographs, a display of tools or found treasures, or a much-loved collection of accessories. Create a room that makes you want to stay another hour in order to finish the drawing, the not-quite-perfect hem, or the household bills. After all, a successful home office is one you're in no hurry to leave.

At Home in the Office

An office perfectly suited to its user satisfies its most deserving client.
The greatest luxury in putting together a home office is that you can
do things your way. This is your chance to bend all the nine-to-five
rules that define office style. Go ahead and indulge your preferences.

To make an office your own calls for thinking outside the "in box". Traditionally defined by a desk, a chair, a phone, a lamp, and storage, a home office need not be a clone of the standard workstation to function well. Forget "business attire" and dress your workroom with furnishings, colours, materials, and accessories that make you feel right at home.

This handsome dormer room employs alternatives to standard office furnishings to provide the crucial amenities of a workspace in a comfortable, personalized setting. Designed for flexibility, the room is divided into three zones: a traditional workstation, a comfortable seating area, and a convenient space for file storage. A laptop computer with wireless connections makes it easy to move from the love seat to the desk and back again; supplies are stored in a tray for easy transport to elsewhere in the room. In lieu of traditional filing cabinets, a set of capacious storage trunks and a ladder-style bookcase add character to the space. Beautifully designed floor and table lamps, such as those you might choose for a living room, offer a pleasing alternative to standard-issue office lighting.

A vintage-style telephone and a table finished in blackboard paint, *left*, make a clever communication centre in the seating area. **A standard white pinboard**, *right*, blends in with the wall to allow the colourful notes and postcards attached to draw attention and serve as eye-catching reminders.

Wireless technology eliminates the need for leads and allows any corner of this simple attic office to be used as a workstation. Keeping supplies in concealed storage, printers in a cupboard, and file boxes tucked under the eaves helps maintain an airy atmosphere. The open framework of a dining or library table offers room on all sides for seating and creates an increased feeling of spaciousness.

A simple home office that offers several work zones accommodates a flexible routine and welcomes many tasks.

A solid, clean-lined library table can easily become a desk when storage is available elsewhere within the room. With castors added for mobility, this desk can be rolled into position under a window or moved against the wall for added floor space. In attics and other tight spots, where it can be a challenge to move furniture, find easy-to-manoeuvre, lightweight pieces that make the most of limited space.

An eclectic mix of furniture and finishes is harmonized by an overall sense of order. With work, seating, and storage zones equally balanced within the room, a muted palette unifies the space and enhances a feeling of airiness.

Design Details

An all-white palette accentuates the height of a pitched ceiling.

An overhead shelf reclaims unused space between the eaves for use as storage.

Placing a desk in the well of a dormer window makes it the focus of the room.

A casual seating arrangement offers an alternative workspace.

A rug neatly defines the work area, making it a room within a room.

Colour Palette

A neutral palette of white, taupe, and brown gives this non-traditional office a clean, professional look. Timeless classics for office decor, neutrals create a calming workroom atmosphere that fosters concentration and focus. Broad expanses of pure white make the whole room – even the tight spaces under the eaves – appear larger. Light brown accents in the upholstered seating area and the soft taupe of the rug add warmth.

Room Plan

Dividing a relatively small room into three distinct zones – the desk, a storage wall, and a seating area that encourages both work and conversation – enhances a feeling of openness in this workspace. While one person works at the desk in the window alcove, another can settle onto the sofa to make phone calls, read the paper, interview clients, or work independently on a laptop. The room's uncluttered layout makes work surfaces and storage easily accessible while facilitating traffic flow. A square light-coloured rug links all three areas visually.

Materials

Oak One of the hardest wood species, oak is both scratch-resistant and long-wearing, making it an ideal choice for hardwood floors.

Blackboard paint The convenience of this paint-on finish makes it easy to transform table tops, walls, and other surfaces into places for jotting notes.

Flat-weave wool Smoothly finished, flat-weave rugs offer a durable, sound-insulating surface that office chairs can move across with ease.

space

However large or small the space, making the most of a work area is about making wise choices. With a little thought, a rarely used corner of the living room or a spare cupboard big enough for a desk and chair can become a compact, private home office. Thinking about space not just in terms of floor area, but with regard to a room's visual impact, traffic patterns, and ease of use, increases your ability to put together a room that works. Be creative with the space available by thinking through the room's main purpose, the needs of

Furnishings that double as storage also benefit a smaller workspace. Filing cubes can serve as seating when fitted with a cushion; a bench that has an open-framework base can hold stacks of books or magazines. Put empty walls to work for you as well. Hang a bulletin board for notes or a pegboard for tools; install wall-mounted shelves or shallow ledges to keep supplies within easy reach.

Options increase in a larger space, but so do considerations of sharing and foot traffic. In a room with lots of users, zone the space into task-specific areas, or pull worktables away from the

Space is what you make of it: a world of its own, a quiet corner, a place to collect your thoughts. It's not how much of it you have, but how well you use it.

each user, and the probable number of regular visitors. Every workspace has its own distinct demands – the expectations for a writer's office and for a family project room are inherently different, and require different layouts. But the best workspaces have certain characteristics in common: a sense of order, an uncluttered work surface, good lighting, and a place to store supplies, paperwork, and other necessities.

In a small space, storage requirements are best satisfied vertically. Use floor-to-ceiling bookcases or stacked cupboards and shelving to keep supplies organized. Suspend pendant lights from the ceiling to free up work surfaces and floor space.

walls for ease of access. Assigning separate storage spaces to each person who uses the room improves the likelihood of quick tidy-ups. With a bit of space planning, filing boxes and other storage systems can be arranged to help direct traffic or establish discrete workstations. An L-shaped arrangement of waist-level worktables easily converts from an office desk to a craft centre.

Remember that space is something of an illusion. A high ceiling can make an average-size room seem generous; a pale, bright wall colour reflects light to make a room seem bigger. Space is not just the area defined by four walls, but the way in which that area is lived in and used.

Working with an Open-Plan Scheme

A spacious loft offers lessons that apply to workrooms large or small. Carve out flexible zones with a central workstation and a mix of built-in and movable pieces. With clear sight lines and 360-degree access, an uncluttered office offers versatility and a feeling of openness.

Whether you work in a large loft with high ceilings and lots of light or a small studio, a feeling of openness is easy to achieve. The trick is to make the most of the layout with a central work area and plenty of well-planned storage.

If your dream is to have an open-plan home office that feels spacious and inviting, try carving out flexible work zones with free-standing furniture that can be reached from all sides. By "floating" your desk or table away from the walls, you provide 360-degree access to a workstation.

To maintain clear sight lines through the room, look for storage with clean lines and an open framework, or pieces that reach mid-level rather than extending all the way from floor to ceiling. Even if you prefer built-in shelves, there's no need to keep them flat against the walls. Here, shelves double as room dividers and still allow plenty of room for foot traffic. Leave open space on shelves to offer glimpses between work zones or into other rooms, or add sculptural elements to be viewed from both sides. In this workspace, architectural models help break up a wall of books and create interesting displays.

Architectural scale models, *left*, arranged in open shelving, are sculptural and intriguing shelf dividers. **Clean lines**, *right*, add to an airy, organized workspace. The sense of spaciousness is reinforced by high ceilings and a white-on-white palette that magnifies the natural light from above.

Here, a floating desk arrangement not only adds to the feeling of spaciousness but actually creates more working area. In place of desks aligned in a traditional manner, a pair of sleek, Perspex-topped dining tables – which can be easily rearranged as needed – form a double-size desk with plenty of room for extra seating. A third table creates an L-shaped return and serves as a corner computer station. An improvised trolley made from pre-cut wood and stainless steel castors makes the computer easily movable.

A desktop covered in Perspex, *above*, functions both as workspace and design portfolio. Inspirational photos are placed beneath the surface and can be changed or updated regularly. A small section is left unadorned to be used as a wipe-clean memo board. **The room's cool white surfaces**, *right*, are enriched by honey-coloured wood floors, a sisal rug, and a rattan chair.

This office's well-planned design makes as imaginative and practical use of the desktop as it does every other bit of the room. A table covered with Perspex provides both a creative display area and a place to keep documents safe from spills.

A lofty, light-filled workspace opens up the possibilities for productive dreamers.

Modular furniture and easily maintained materials make for versatile and user-friendly spaces. Ambient and natural lighting, combined with swing-arm desk lamps that can be adjusted for each task, provide light for every work zone.

Simple trolleys can be rigged to store and transport computer equipment or heavy items like filing boxes. Adding castors to any piece of furniture is an easy way to double its usefulness and increase flexibility. Use adjustable stools as extra seating. They can be tucked away under the desktop to keep pathways clear for foot traffic or rolling chairs.

A multi-purpose desktop, *left*, provides zones for a computer station, a light box, and a cutting mat. **A well-designed workroom**, *right*, multiplies the number of available workstations with a strategic arrangement of tables.

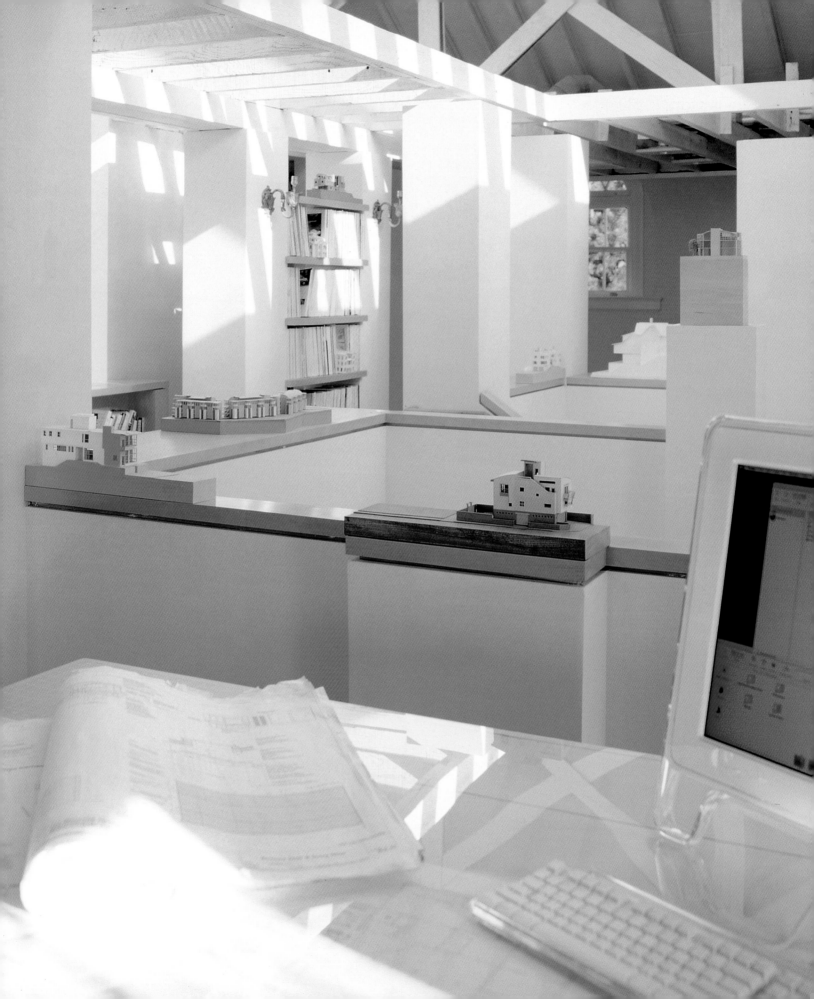

Design Details

Keeping tall furnishings to the periphery helps maintain sight lines.

Filing boxes lined up along an unused wall provide out-of-the-way storage.

Shelves accessible from two sides make the most of a narrow space.

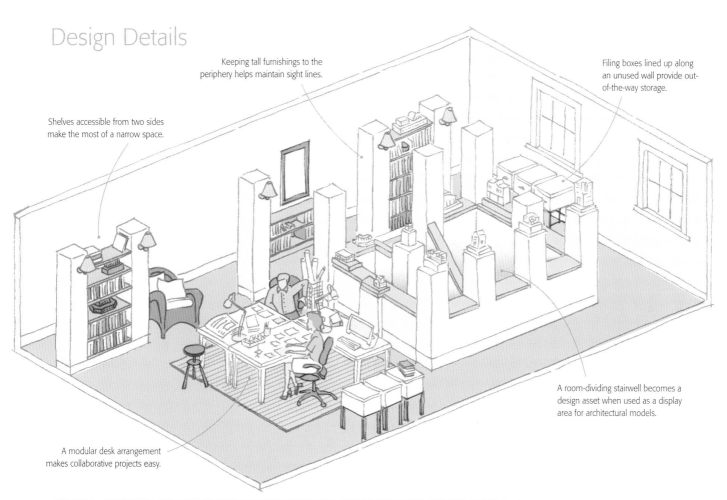

A room-dividing stairwell becomes a design asset when used as a display area for architectural models.

A modular desk arrangement makes collaborative projects easy.

Colour Palette

White can be warm or cool, and the tint you choose subtly affects everything in the room. The warm white on the walls of this room contains yellow undertones, which complement the clear honey colour of the wood floors and shelving. The cool white of the desk is tinged with blue, making it a nice complement to the brushed metal desk accessories. Accents of black, in the mesh desk chairs and swivel stool, add a modern contrast.

Room Plan

This office design makes a virtue of the stairwell that divides the space into two sections. The front section is the largest and contains the principal workstation. The remainder of the space is divided into storage and traffic zones. Parallel "corridors", defined by several pairs of bookcases, provide access to research books and files from both sides and allow traffic flow along the length of the room. Free-floating desks follow suit, and offer 360-degree access to workstations, encouraging collaborative projects and emphasizing a sense of spaciousness.

Materials

Perspex A trademarked name for sheets of clear acrylic, this synthetic material is lightweight, easy to clean, and makes a versatile and practical work surface.

Sisal A flexible plant fibre, sisal is often woven into durable, textured rugs that hide dirt and resist stains.

Steel A favourite office material and a high-tech classic, steel is iron alloyed with a small percentage of carbon for strength.

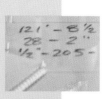

A Working Guest Room

For many of us, a home office must double as a welcoming guest room. To find a proper balance, look for discreet storage, versatile furniture, and thoughtful amenities – an inviting chair, a stack of books, and adjustable lighting that suits both diligent workers and overnight visitors.

Not all of us have the luxury of a dedicated home office. Many of us have workrooms that must also serve an added function, whether as a den, a media room, or a spare bedroom for guests. In the case of the latter, you'll want an office with adaptable furnishings that are both comfortable for overnight visitors and practical for working. Keep in mind the needs of your guests when setting up a workroom, but be careful not to let one function overrule another. Work areas should be balanced with sleeping spaces so that the room encourages both creativity and relaxation.

A fresh coat of white paint on the walls makes a welcome backdrop for a room meant to serve more than one use, especially when space is at a premium. Add soft accents with inviting elements like a warm, textured rug, twill loose covers, and white cotton diaphanous curtains. Choose simple but cosy furnishings. Streamlined forms increase a feeling of spaciousness. Decorative storage keeps office files from intruding upon guests. A pyramid of vintage suitcases, or an old wardrobe refitted as a computer station, lends a whimsical touch.

Stacked canvas suitcases, *left and right*, make an amusing display for a treasured collection of pulp fiction and mystery novels while doubling as storage for files, tax records, and seasonal clothes. Colourful old-fashioned luggage labels indicate the contents of each for easy retrieval.

Even the busiest home office can be quickly transformed into a guest room if you have adaptable furnishings and a decor that appeals to both purposes. A classic truckle bed can discreetly hide storage in its oversized "drawer" without sacrificing floor space or comfort. A simple white table top tucked under a window can go from desk to breakfast nook as needed.

Look for dual-purpose furniture and creative ways to meet the demands of both home office and guest room.

In this restful guest room, files and office supplies are tucked out of sight but remain easy to retrieve when needed. In place of filing cabinets, the desk is fitted with a hanging canvas storage panel that can be folded up and put away. Additional storage is found in the stack of old-fashioned suitcases that can be conveniently reconfigured to form a bedside table. A pile of reference books acts as a telephone table between the desk and a loose-covered reading chair.

A corner workspace, *left*, keeps the office zone contained. An abundant supply of cushions makes a truckle day-bed welcoming and comfortable for overnight guests. **A shadow box**, *right*, lined with enlargements of pages from pulp novels, serves as an enticing bookshelf and a unique display.

Colour Palette

A generous application of white in this compact guest room/study enlarges the space visually and opens up the possibilities for display. The simple palette provides a clean backdrop for dual-purpose furnishings. With the walls, bed, desk and armchair painted or upholstered in white, the tower of leather suitcases in every shade of brown – from mocha to caramel to chocolate – makes a dramatic contrast. The varied brown hues of a natural fibre rug tie the room's decor together.

Materials

Abaca Woven from the strong fibres of a banana-plant leafstalk, abaca rugs make a fine choice for a home office that also doubles as a guest room – adding a subtle pattern and natural texture underfoot for comfort and warmth.

Painted plaster Durable and sound-absorbent, painted plaster is easy to clean and can be repainted to quickly change the look of a room. Walls of smooth plaster painted white or any pale hue will reflect light and give a small room a feeling of spaciousness.

Vintage suitcases Canvas and leather cases can be easily found at flea markets and are ideal solutions when floor space is at a premium: stacked on the floor or arranged in a graduated tower, they perform double duty as whimsical display art and storage.

Almost as deep as it is wide, the built-in desktop is positioned between the room's two windows to make the most of natural light. Constructed of a solid door that's been cut to size and painted the same white as the bed, it's suspended between the bed and the wall, leaving plenty of floor space for storing files or luggage underneath. A wall-mounted swivel lamp saves space and provides task lighting for both the room's functions: it's a desk lamp over the work area and is close enough to the bed for late-night reading.

A four-pocket canvas panel, *left*, is affixed to the underside of the desk, leaving the surface free for work and display while keeping floor space free for file storage or a luggage rack. **A collection of vintage typewriters**, *above*, serves as witty holders for photos.

An Everyday Office

A small desk at the top of the stairs offers a tidy place to lay down your keys and post. It also makes a convenient spot to pay the bills, write letters, or find things quickly on your way out.

At the end of a long day, sometimes all that's needed is a place to hang your coat and drop the post (and your weary self). Here, a scaled-down roll-top desk provides designated storage for papers, outgoing post, accessories, and keys. Versatile furniture pieces with pull-out or fold-down writing surfaces do twice the work as a place to manage bills and the grab-and-go traffic of a household.

A fresh white palette, *opposite*, keeps things looking tidy. A desk scaled to the space, *left*, is outfitted with clever containers, including a vintage bath-sponge holder for the post. Nautical hardware, *above*, rounds up keys.

How to Find Space

When space is your scarcest commodity, think like a boatbuilder – or a graduate student. Improvisation and a bit of clever planning can produce a compact desk from little more than a shelf and a pair of brackets. Create a study from an unused cupboard by installing a shallow desktop with a few shelves above. Make a reading nook under a staircase with a cosy chair and a sconce light. Limited space invites a few shrewd design tricks: find small-scale furnishings that can be folded shut; mount lights under a shelf to save desktop space; employ a light-coloured palette to increase the perceived space; above all, keep it simple.

A low coffee table is a cosy desk, *above*, when equipped with all the amenities of an office. Easy-to-carry filing boxes, a compact laptop computer, breadboard extensions, and a sturdy tray make finding space to work a breeze.

A shallow bookcase, *right*, takes up little floor space but is wide enough to hold all the basics of a snug bedside office. Its narrow profile transforms a sliver of space into the perfect place for making morning calls, scheduling appointments, or catching up with friends.

An inviting alcove, *opposite*, takes advantage of leftover space in a kitchen. The marble desk surface integrates the work zone with the rest of the room and is just wide enough for a laptop computer and a cookery book – a perfect combination for finding and filing new recipes. A slender but comfortable chair can be pushed flush with the desktop when not in use.

5

colour

1:25PM
00-0001 001 JUL 14/03
#31119 CASH A
CLERK

Colour is personal, and powerful. It affects mood, productivity – even our appetites. It can soothe or stimulate, brighten or energize, and even inspire creativity. Some of us like a lot of it, some only a little, but faced with a towering display of paint colour samples, just about every one of us becomes indecisive and starts wishing for a personal colour consultant.

The good news about choosing colour for a home office is that there are no rules. You're the boss. If red is the colour that energizes you, treat yourself to four walls of bold crimson – or accent up and help minimize flaws in plaster walls or highlight beautiful mouldings. Bright colours tend to draw objects into the foreground; quieter shades allow them to retreat into the background. Dark colours can visually reduce the size of a room, but many a tiny space has been turned into a perfect jewel box when painted in a rich, saturated hue and lit with lots of accent lamps.

Remember, too, that natural and artificial light both affect colour, so it always makes sense to try out a colour in a room. To see how a colour really looks in your space throughout the day, applying

Colour gives a workroom warmth and personality. For a completely new look that's uniquely your own, nothing changes a room's atmosphere more than colour.

an all-white workroom with a single scarlet lampshade. If navy blue is a hue that inspires you to succeed, then by all means, put the power of that colour to work for you in a home office.

Colour can be used to set the mood in a workspace or announce a theme, to boldly project or subtly accent, as when a border of palest green quietly draws the eye to a built-in bookcase. It can transform second-hand furniture into one-of-a-kind treasures or bring uniformity to a collection of mismatched pieces and newer furnishings.

That said, awareness of some of colour's effects can help you make successful choices. Use light colours – and especially white – to open a room true paint samples is the best test, if you have time. For the most useful preview, paint a patch on one or two walls, then observe the colour in both daylight and lamplight to make sure you like it at all times of day. If your space is small, adopt this designer trick for adding colour without dominating a room: paint one wall in a vibrant colour and leave the others white or neutral.

Because colour is so personal, a neutral palette often makes the most sense for a shared workspace. But the determining factor in choosing colour should always be personal taste, matched to setting and purpose. There is no "right" colour for a workspace, only the right colour for you.

Putting Colour to Work

There's a temptation to forgo luscious colour in favour of more serious hues in a workspace. But bright colours offer much-needed energy, and jewel tones inspire. Add sunny colours to your office, and there's no need to feel like you're missing out while working indoors on a lovely day.

Colour theory holds that strong reds and oranges evoke high energy, speed the flow of blood to the brain, and increase metabolism. Instinct tells us that nothing improves mood or restores a faltering sense of optimism better than a sunny day, which leads one to wonder why all workspaces aren't bathed in a golden yellow coat of paint and fitted with crimson accents for inspiration.

A fearless abundance of colour can be the defining element in your workroom, as it is in this simply furnished home office. A sophisticated shade of golden yellow makes a perfect backdrop for a spare and sculptural collection of classic furnishings in wood tones and distressed finishes. Window frames, skirting boards, and mouldings are painted a crisp, glossy white to accentuate the colourful walls and reinforce the room's architectural details. The colour palette enhances the welcoming atmosphere, and gently worn finishes create a sense of informality in this richly detailed office. Window blinds in complementary ochre, rust, and natural ticking stripes add a softening touch to the space.

The play of a weathered zinc desk, *left*, against yellow makes a dramatic still life of an ordinary office configuration. A richly hued kilim rug adds a layer of warmth and texture, in keeping with the vivid colours of the room and its colourful accents. **A beautifully worn wooden ladder**, *right*, is put to imaginative use as a pinboard, organizer, and newspaper rack.

Here, the chosen shade of yellow is just neutral enough to give free rein to small touches of bright red and deep brown without being overwhelmed. A saturated hue can both stand up to and play off against bold patterns. The geometric repeat of the kilim rug is echoed in the ticking stripe of the Roman blinds and the collection of red, brown, and olive green storage containers. This rich colour palette yields a workspace with a sunny yet serious disposition.

Colour and texture serve as the primary accents in a home office that is simply furnished and boldly accessorized.

For a relatively small space, this home office takes advantage of all its assets. The streamlined desk is positioned between the two large windows to make the most of cross breezes and natural lighting. A compact reading area takes up the remaining space with a leather armchair and a simple side table. Colourful accents unify these spaces and add impact.

Powerful colour goes a long way in a workroom, and simple furnishings like a classic leather armchair, a clean-lined table, and a hanging brass lamp are set off by the room's warm and sophisticated palette.

Colour Palette

A rich palette of warm yellows, reds, and browns extends from the floor to the ceiling, bringing energy and elegance to this cosy home study. Golden yellow walls glow with the light throughout the day. All around is an interplay of jewel tones and rich textures: scarlet accents in the chair and on the bookshelf, magenta and amber notes in the kilim rug, and burnished tones of ochre and russet in the fabric of the Roman blinds and the ticking stripes of the cushion.

Colour need not coat the walls or show up in bold applications such as furnishings to make an impact. Whether old, new, purchased, or inherited, storage containers in a range of colours and materials are both decorative and practical in a workroom. Here, a graduated bookshelf forms an evocative display of shapes and colours, with reds, tans, and mottled browns nestled together on the shelves. The unexpected mix of cigar boxes, cardboard storage cubes, cash boxes, and vintage leather overnight cases adds character to a wall of shelving while enhancing an already rich palette.

Mixed, matched, and stacked, *left*, this eclectic storage solution and display unit could be easily adapted to almost any workroom or colour scheme. **An assortment of boxes in leather, wood, and metal,** *above*, is a striking alternative to standard office storage and comprises a collection worth putting on display.

Materials

Kilim Originated by nomadic tribes in Afghanistan, Iran, Iraq, and Turkey, kilims are especially durable flat-weave wool rugs that were used to cover sand floors. They are coveted for their warm colour palettes and beautiful graphic designs.

Brass An alloy of zinc and copper metals produces gleaming brass. Sealed with a finish to prevent tarnish and discourage fingerprints, brass lampshades are a practical choice that add elegance and shine to a workspace or dining area.

Zinc A metallic element of surprising strength and durability, zinc has an initial sheen that is similar to stainless steel's, but it weathers to a matt, blue-grey patina over time. Prized for its softly worn finish, zinc has made its way into items including desks, tables, and worktops.

How to Add Colour

Bringing colour to an office or workspace is one of the quickest ways to alter its atmosphere. You can brighten a room that gets little sun with a coat of golden yellow paint, warm a north-facing room with a luscious shade of red-orange, or create a calming mood with a palette of cool blues and greens. Colour can add energy to a space (think of the associations with bold reds, yellows, oranges) or sophistication (consider rich browns, heathered greys, polished black). Whether it's the defining element in the room or a recurring accent, colour can inspire you and steer you towards your best work.

Empty candle votives filled with pencils, *above*, suggest cool ocean breezes with their sea-glass tones and matt finish. **This fabric-covered desk blotter**, *right*, makes a quick transformation possible. With a metre of fabric and a bit of glue, you can switch colours to suit the season, your mood, or a change in office decor. Sometimes the simplest accessories can provide just the right touch of colour in a room or inspire you to rethink its current palette.

Walls painted in unexpected colours, *left*, are the most dramatic colour statement you can make, but are also the biggest leap for many of us to take. It often helps to start small with a colour you are drawn to and see how you like it: hanging a piece of brilliantly coloured fabric on a wall will give you a preview without your having to make an all-out commitment to repainting. **Elegant accessories and richly coloured rugs**, *below left*, add a bright spot of colour to a room and are often enough to change its sensibility without any further additions. **Painting the insides of in and out boxes**, *below*, in a favourite hue lends a touch of whimsy to an otherwise serious desktop.

texture

Texture is what nature guarantees, and what our senses seek indoors as well as out. Texture is most easily understood as the feel of things: the nub of natural linen, the cool slide of a marble table top, the smooth grain of a mahogany desk, the welcome softness of a thick rug underfoot. Texture is to colour as touch is to sight – each works in synergy with the other. Texture is highlighted by juxtaposing materials: a stainless steel worktop fitted on weathered cupboards; a pair of matched reading chairs, one upholstered in smooth leather, its mate outfitted

You can also highlight texture by playing off the expected: natural wood against a lacquer finish, silk curtains against brick walls, a stainless steel book trolley against an antique maple desk.

When choosing basic pieces for the office, consider using alternative materials and finishes to add variety to the room's mix. Filing cabinets in wood or a brushed steel finish make a stylish change from standard painted metal units. A linen table runner in lieu of a plain blotter softens the edges of a traditional desktop. And just think what a double coat of red lacquer on a weathered

Texture works in subtle ways to bring life to a room. It's variety and surprise – the pleasure of materials that look good, feel good, and offer appealing contrasts.

in raw silk. Texture is variation, subtlety, the pleasure of the unexpected: old abutting new, rough highlighting smooth. It is the contrast between a polished wood floor and the kilim runner laid across it, between the brass base of a lamp and the woven linen of its shade.

In a workroom, as in any other room in the house, use texture to stimulate the senses while maintaining the overall harmony of the space. A white-on-white palette might include several related tones of white, for example, with room accents in a range of textures: a white-on-white draughtboard wool rug, bleached twill loose covers, a glossy painted desk, a whitewashed bookcase.

work surface might do for your mood when you flip on the lights some grey February morning.

Supplies are the mainstay of any workroom, so equip your office with a rich range of textured accessories that make art out of the everyday. A palette of beautiful textures makes work tools a pleasure to look at and use. Stacked books can be weighted with a smooth fieldstone; files of paperwork can be set in woven baskets that are both beautiful and practical. So go ahead, line up your reference texts with a rusted iron anchor as a bookend. All the materials you choose in a workroom are there for good reason: they are part of the texture of your working life.

Planning a Garden Workroom

In a rustic garden shed, as in nature, a range of textures soothes the mind and calms the senses. Use the subtle interplay between man-made and natural, between sleek and weathered surfaces, between metal and wood, to play up textures and emphasize the simple beauty of everyday things.

Some rooms seem to spring to life almost without human assistance, a perfect synergy of site and purpose resulting in a space that seems meant to be. An eye for natural beauty that needs little improving is one ingredient in creating such a space; restraint is another. This storybook potting shed yields lessons in textural contrast and simple beauty that can be easily applied to any workspace.

In this setting, where organization is at a premium, subtle variations in texture provide visual interest while promoting an overall sense of order. The contrast of worn surfaces against sleek ones works especially well within a monochromatic colour palette. Experiment with subtle variations of your favourite colour in a range of textures. Combine distressed finishes with high-gloss ones, ribbed or piquéd fabrics with flat-weave cottons or the smoothest silk. Choose tools and accessories in natural materials and put them to work alongside enamelled steel storage. Just imagine how a woven basket for desktop supplies provides welcome contrast to a computer, a sculptural ceramic bowl makes a lovely vessel for daily post, or a beautifully aged deck chair offsets a brand-new garden umbrella.

A shiny aluminium tub filled with sand, *left*, offers a safe berth for a set of wood-handled garden tools and a lesson in creative storage. **A garden umbrella and a timeworn Adirondack chair**, *right*, turn a patch of flowers into an inviting outdoor sitting room.

The possibilities of texture come alive in a gardener's haven. Consistent use of a few materials – galvanized steel, painted wood, white enamelware – creates a unifying framework within which variety has full rein. Apply the lessons of this rustic potting shed to your own workspace. Use subtle shifts of colour to catch the eye, and create variations on a theme to call attention to kinships of pattern and shape. Here, spherical shapes are repeated in glass and ceramic, and baskets are unified by a simple coat of white paint.

Galvanized buckets and trays, *above*, are classic choices for the garden but could just as readily house pencils, stationery, or bills on a desktop.
A palette of contrasting textures, *right*, is most visible in the potting shed's storage centre that runs the length of the wall: painted wood punctuated by unpainted patches; enamelled, galvanized, and distressed metal containers; glass jars and window panes that allow sunlight into the room.

In a workspace where potting compost, seedlings, and water are an integral part of the supply inventory, keeping things tidy can be a challenge. Beginning with a palette of textures that will help camouflage everyday wear and tear, choose materials that match the room's purpose. Stainless and galvanized work surfaces are durable and easy to clean. Airtight, enamelled steel bins protect seeds from wetness and humidity.

To create a calming place for work, mix textures the same way a gardener mixes textures in nature.

The most successful workrooms are as much about a passion for the task as the need to accomplish it. When planning your personal office, go all out on the touches that breathe life into the space and express its special meaning to you. Placing plant labels in the framework of a chicken-wire cupboard keeps them organized while indulging happy memories of your holiday in Provence.

A chicken-wire cupboard, *left*, holds white plaster topiaries, adding a touch of charm to the room's rustic look. A hessian-covered pinboard, *right*, draws the eye to favourite garden images and a display of antique padlocks.

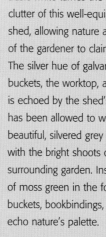

Colour Palette

Basic white tames the necessary clutter of this well-equipped potting shed, allowing nature and the tools of the gardener to claim centre stage. The silver hue of galvanized metal buckets, the worktop, and portable trays is echoed by the shed's exterior, which has been allowed to weather. The beautiful, silvered grey contrasts nicely with the bright shoots of green in the surrounding garden. Inside, accents of moss green in the form of metal buckets, bookbindings, and young plants echo nature's palette.

Galvanized metal cladding is one of the most distinctive and practical surfaces for a workroom. Inexpensive and durable, it can be custom cut to fit almost any surface and makes both an easy-care alternative to wood and an appealing partner to it texturally. Wood-handled tools hang within quick reach, while oversize galvanized bins under the worktop store lawn-care materials in bulk. The vibrant green of the table top terrarium adds colour and texture – elements that bring warmth and interest to every workspace.

Galvanized storage bins, *left*, can be used indoors for potting, outdoors for lawn and garden care, or brought into a home office for use as filing and storage bins. **Garden supplies like compost and fertilizer**, *above*, are best stored out of direct sunlight.

Materials

Galvanized metal Rustproof galvanized metal is highly valued for its low cost, light weight, flexibility, and good looks. Custom-cut sheets can make a durable, waterproof work surface for any table.

Enamelware Sealed with a thin coating of enamel that's fused to the metal vessel, enamelware comes in variations of mottled graniteware or sleek solid colours and is among the most practical and pleasing of containers. Dents and nicks seem only to improve its character.

Terracotta Italian for "baked earth", this type of clay is the preferred choice of gardeners because its porousness helps plants retain moisture between waterings. The shapely pots are as well suited for holding desk supplies as they are for herbs and houseplants.

A nest of wooden bowls, *below*, makes a desktop catch-all for bulldog clips, drawing pins, and other small office items and is a handsome reminder to leave the office-supply catalogue at work. A wooden rice measure from Asia, *right*, is subdivided with simple rubber bands to keep pencils, bulldog clips, and drawing tools neatly separated. Antique cast-iron finials, *below right*, serve as elegant paperweights and subtle directionals for in and out boxes.

How to Add Natural Texture

There's no easier way to enliven a home office than to introduce the shapes and textures of nature. In a workspace obliged to accommodate the industrial edges of a desk, computer, fax, and phone, the simple beauty of natural materials and timeworn objects lends visual interest and aesthetic pleasure. It provides inspiration for creative endeavours and welcome distraction from everyday tasks. The patina of polished wood, the smooth feel of a river stone used as a paperweight, baskets of wicker or woven willow all add warmth and depth to a room, softening its man-made edges and gently blurring the distinction between home work and home life.

A wooden carpenter's toolbox, *left*, fitted out as a desktop supply kit, is a thing of beauty in its own right, and appealing enough to be used in any room of the house (substitute recipe cards and a chequebook in the kitchen, notepaper and letter-writing supplies in the living room). **A softly textured basket of woven rush**, *above*, adds a touch of craftsmanship to a room while storing newspapers and keeping them neatly organized with a dividing length of twine.

furnishings

Furniture makes things happen in a room. It creates scale, adds comfort, defines style, and facilitates the room's purpose. Whether choosing furniture for a small family project room or outfitting a lofty painter's studio, think about the specific items that will make the room function the way you want it to.

As with any room in the house, it's best to start with the main pieces first. Does a classic desk with multiple drawers make most sense for the way you work? Or, do you need a free-standing worktable the whole family can gather around?

desk. Once you've decided on the type of desk and chair that best suits your needs, start thinking about the satellite pieces you'll need: book-shelves, filing cabinets, computer trolleys, reading chairs. Match practicality with personal style, and don't limit yourself to "office" furniture, especially when carving a workspace from a guest bedroom or living room. If you're furnishing a family project centre, keep an eye out for old library tables at flea markets. If your work includes sketching, visit on-line auctions for drawing boards and other artist-specific equipment. With

Choose comfortable furnishings that satisfy your work habits and the needs of the room. Add unusual pieces that reflect your style. That's all there is to know.

Perhaps a dining table with movable filing cabinets underneath is what best suits your style. Next, decide how your desk will work within the overall plan. Do you enjoy being able to look out a window, or are you more likely to stay focussed facing a working wall with a calendar, pinboard, and notes? A central workstation, around which traffic can flow, is ideal for some workspaces. Decide whether open-plan is best for you, or if you prefer working at a desk tucked in a corner.

The single best investment you can make in a workspace is a sturdy and supportive desk chair. Opt for the highest-quality chair you can afford, and be sure that it adjusts to the height of your

the vision of your ideal workspace clear in your mind's eye, you'll more easily recognize the furnishings that will both do the job and delight you when you look up, mid-thought, halfway through a project or assignment.

Finally, think about how you really spend the day. Everyone has a special work routine, so assess yours and furnish your space accordingly. Do you like a nap now and then? Pace the floor when you're thinking something through? Well-chosen pieces, like a day-bed that doubles as seating for clients, or a plush, patterned rug, can make all the difference in creating a workspace that's uniquely yours.

Basics of a Welcoming Workspace

A stylish set-up with flexible furniture and versatile lighting can bring just the right level of polish to a workspace, while keeping it warm and welcoming. And when your home office is used for meetings or courting prospective clients, no detail is too small to consider.

A home office doesn't have to be grand to be an inviting space you'd be proud to show clients, but it does have to be organized and stylish. If your office is one that hosts even the occasional client, keep in mind that furnishings and accessories always make a strong first impression.

That doesn't mean a working home office must conform to corporate style rules. At home, you're free to arrange your space according to the way you work best. In the pursuit of a comfortable business sensibility, size matters less than function. Set up your workstation so that reference materials, files, printer, and phone are situated nearby. You don't want an office that looks organized to visitors but requires you to jump up from your desk every time you need something. A separate area for entertaining clients, even if it's a small space, often makes a friendlier, more polished impression than meetings hosted at your desk.

When choosing a colour palette, select hues that harmonize with the rest of your space. This office is a good example. Off-white trim and pale citrus walls create a fresh backdrop for warm wood tones and lots of natural light.

Rough-hewn wooden stools, *left*, serve as seating or side tables, as needed. **A triangular shelf tower**, *right*, displays sculptural artwork and keeps reference materials and samples readily available. Movable furnishings are angled towards the display for comfortable viewing.

To create an uncluttered impression and a space that feels open to creativity, keep large pieces to a minimum and choose modular pieces or those that serve more than one function. Furniture that is wall-mounted or pieces that stand on narrow legs help make a space feel larger and more open. If you have frequent meetings, another option is a desk that quickly closes to conceal works-in-progress when clients are scheduled to arrive.

A home office that signals creativity and professionalism invites guests as well as clients.

An organized workspace also requires a flexible lighting plan. A hanging globe light, connected to a dimmer switch, creates a range of soft ambient light for the entire room. Gallery lights positioned on the wall above the desk offer adjustable task lighting without casting a glare on the computer screen. Shutters on the windows offer the same protection.

A palm leaf and papyrus grass frond, *left*, in oversize curvaceous glass vases make stylish substitutes for standard office plants. A clever desktop system, *right*, has a naturalist bent: just for fun, labelled stones help signal incoming and outgoing files. Furniture in a palette of light wood tones produces a harmonious effect.

Displaying personal collections and photos expresses your creativity while making your office truly feel like home. Here, a pinboard propped up behind the desk, a painting held by a simple clip frame, and favourite postcards form an artistic but orderly backdrop to the spacious work area.

A pared-down suite offers a desk area for creating great work and a sitting room for presenting it.

Key to this office's versatility is the ability to move furnishings between the office space and the client area across the hall. Convertible pieces can adjust to create different configurations, whether you're working on a project or hosting a client meeting. Matching sectional chairs move together to form a settee, and a standard sawhorse table serves as both desk and conference table. The shelving in this room doubles as a portable display: hinged at the top with planks balanced between the rungs, it folds flat for easy storage.

The open framework of a sawhorse desk and triangular shelving defines the clean look of this practical office set-up. New pieces like an Aeron desk chair and classic shapes like the plywood chair in the client area reveal the owner's style while maintaining a professional atmosphere.

Design Details

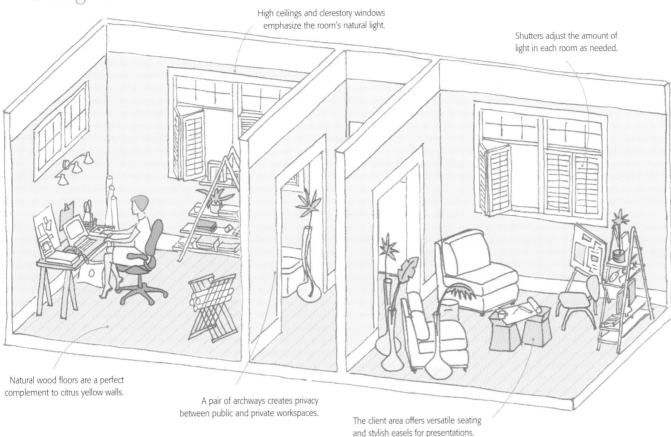

High ceilings and clerestory windows emphasize the room's natural light.

Shutters adjust the amount of light in each room as needed.

Natural wood floors are a perfect complement to citrus yellow walls.

A pair of archways creates privacy between public and private workspaces.

The client area offers versatile seating and stylish easels for presentations.

Colour Palette

Short of making a sunny spot outdoors into your office, it's hard to imagine a better setting for a garden-lover's workroom than this serene indoor colourscape. The combination of citrus yellow walls with the deep green of the graceful palm fronds evokes a tropical paradise, and a sense of high style simultaneously. Honey-coloured stained wood floors and furniture in mellow shades of light brown enhance the natural look.

Room Plan

Adjacent rooms separated by a small open hallway make a home office as comfortable for working as it is welcoming to clients. The room on the left is set up as a working studio, with a minimum of clutter and plenty of natural light for close work. The stylishly furnished room on the right, where clients are received, offers plenty of room for displaying designs and talking through ideas, while showcasing a landscape architect's design sensibility. A shared colour scheme and open doorways connect the two rooms and make the suite seem more spacious.

Materials

Oak A dense hardwood, oak is widely used in house and furniture construction. These re-planed floorboards were salvaged from old beams.

Twill A tightly woven fabric recognizable by its diagonal grain, twill is a versatile and durable choice for loose covers.

Pine A pale softwood popular for shelving, pine comes in several grades. The knottier the grain, the more rustic the effect. Pine can be easily stained or sanded and left unfinished.

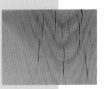

Compact Corner Office

A sense of scale gives a small home office
a neat, uncrowded feeling. White paint and
contemporary details visually expand the
space while desks on castors offer flexibility.

Compact furnishings and an all-white
palette can do wonders for a small
space. The open atmosphere of this
family office owes much to its clever
pieces, chosen for their flexibility
and low profiles. Trim desks set on
narrow legs and castors save space
in a compact room. A simple palette
of white and black helps reduce
visual clutter, while reflective materials
enhance the airiness of the space.
All furniture in the room is arranged
to make the most of the natural light.

A clear Perspex desk chair, *left*, practically
disappears, contributing to the room's sense of
openness. **Labelled storage bins**, *above*, neatly
reveal their contents. **Colourful magnets**, *right*,
post reminders directly on metal furnishings.

GREAT ESCAPES JUDITH MILLER

THE GARDENS OF FLORENCE ALBRIZZI/POOL

Paris Interiors

North Carolina Architecture

The Middle Ages

PEREIRE AND VAN ZUYLEN

O California! Vincent Scully Mills

Irving Penn   PASSAGE

MAGRITTE

Serene Style for a Bedroom Study

An office that shares space with a bedroom should be both inspiring and restful. In this light-filled room, an uncluttered work area is set into a generous window bay. Consistency in style throughout the room creates a soothing, visually integrated effect.

When necessity – or preference – calls for locating a home office in a bedroom, special considerations come into play. It's helpful to create a distinction between the sleeping area and the working area. The two should be well defined but visually harmonious, linked by a shared palette and related styles. This is the place to put comfort and preference first when choosing furniture. Try a handsome dining table or drawing board in place of a traditional desk. As sleek as it is decorative, a table provides plenty of work surface while preserving the intimacy of a bedroom.

Well-organized storage clears space for carefully selected personal items and streamlined office accessories. Files and other paperwork should be concealed in drawers or cupboards in order to maintain a peaceful atmosphere. Choose lamps and desk accessories with warm textures and clean lines to ease the transition from relaxing to working. Elegant furnishings, like a classic upholstered chair, and a polished desk and bench, within a rich colour palette, define an area that is as soothing to look at as it is rewarding to work in.

A wooden bench, *left*, serves as a low bookshelf, accessible to both sleeping and working areas. **Subtle touches of colour**, *right*, from resin boxes in amber and yellow, energize the work area in a room otherwise dressed with a neutral palette of brown, sepia, and white.

A richly textured natural palette of pure white and deep brown links the two main areas, keeping both zones of the room in visual harmony. Layers of silk, velvet, leather, and mohair on the bed and a tone-on-tone area rug define a luxurious sleeping space. Polished wood floors, a loose-covered desk chair, and crisp white Roman blinds outfit the work area. A horizontal bench placed in front of the desk displays a book collection while providing a necessary line of demarcation between sleeping and working spaces.

A subtly patterned area rug, *left*, softens the mood of the room and helps define zones for sleeping and working. **Sheets of Italian manuscript paper**, *above*, serve as elegant dust covers for stacks of books. The room's many repetitions – of books, manuscript paper, stones, and vases – along horizontal lines create an orderly and tranquil atmosphere.

Middle Ages

FRANCE   PEREIRE AND VAN ZUYLEN

O California!   Vincent Starr Mills

Irving Penn   PASSAGE

MAGRITTE

Colour Palette

In a room of muted and closely aligned hues, a splash of colour, however small, works to brilliant effect. A serene and layered colourscape composed of rich brown furnishings and fabrics, with soft, ivory accessories, is set against a backdrop of crisp white walls and windows. The deep hues help define the sleeping and work areas. A pair of handmade resin containers in vivid tones of amber draws the eye to a small spot of colour on the desktop, where they reflect daylight streaming in from the alcove's windows.

A minimalist approach to desk accessories helps preserve peace of mind in a bedroom office. In this space, where horizontal lines are emphasized and repeated, clutter is kept to a minimum with the aid of technology: a sleek laptop computer (with a CD burner for storing records on disk instead of paper) leaves plenty of work surface free. Create a personalized desktop tableau with non-traditional office accessories, like a corduroy table runner in lieu of a desk blotter, or a decorative clear glass accent lamp. The overall effect is a workstation that's stylish enough to double as a dressing table.

Materials

Mohair Woven from the long, wavy hair of Angora goats, with cotton or silk often mixed in, mohair is one of the softest and most luxurious materials to place close to your skin. It is also twice as strong as wool.

Velvet Traditionally woven from silk, cotton, or wool, velvet has a raised pile, which consists of rows of loops that are cut to create a plush texture. Both delicate and surprisingly durable, velvet is one of the world's most practical indulgences. Unusual and luxurious in an office, velvet lends a regal warmth to any room.

Wood Natural wood flooring helps absorb sound and retains the warmth of the sun, making it a wise choice for a sunny study or bedroom. Its rich hue and interesting grain also warm the room visually.

Milk glass votives, *left*, hold delicate Casablanca lilies to soften the look of the desktop. **A shallow oval metal basket**, *above*, acts as both an out tray and a textural display.

Classic Desk Layouts

The traditional set-up of a desk may seem non-negotiable, but with modular office furnishings, personal preference is easily satisfied. Some like their desk drawers on the right-hand side, others prefer them on the left. A symmetrical set-up might be best for a desk that's shared, or an L-shaped arrangement better for multi-tasking. Whatever your specific work needs, there's a set-up that will bring everything together, and it's worth an afternoon of puzzling it out to find the one that best suits you.

The popular L-shaped desk arrangement, *opposite*, becomes a cosy U with the addition of a bookcase for housing files and supplies. As streamlined as a galley kitchen, the enclosed U puts everything within reach. If you tend to settle in for the day, it's a perfect set-up.

The "floating" desk arrangement, *above right*, leaves plenty of room to roam and is probably a better option if you like to push back from your desk and stare at the ceiling, or take frequent walks around the room. It also has less of an office feel to it, making it a good choice for a living-room or bedroom home office.

A back-to-back H configuration, *right*, gives peace of mind to multi-taskers as it permits shifting from one desk to another as needed. It's a useful configuration for a shared office as well, offering a separate station for each worker while taking up a minimum of space.

How to Reinvent a Desk

There are few furnishings more straightforward and simple than an office desk, but take a moment to explore the decorative possibilities and the results may surprise you. For a work surface as personal and idiosyncratic as you choose to make it, dispense with the idea of a standard-issue desk. There's no need to settle for corporate-style accessories, and certainly no reason to sit down to a desktop of grey laminate, when what makes you really happy is working at a table covered with your favourite tablecloth. It's your space, so feel free to fashion a lap desk from a breakfast tray, or a letter-writing station from a step stool.

A sheet of clear glass or acrylic, *above*, turns any work surface into a protected photo gallery or inspiration board. Lining some of the desktop with pale paper or leaving part of the surface free gives you space to scribble erasable notes to yourself or jot down numbers or appointments. With this set-up, the desk becomes an all-in-one work surface, portfolio, bulletin board, and message centre. **A simple wood desk with a tempered glass inset**, *right*, lets you keep important drawings, phone lists, or blueprints protected yet visible under an easy-to-clean work surface.

A double-drawered grain bin, *above left*, makes a convenient catch-all for newspapers and magazines, files, or office supplies. Attached to the underside of a desk or simply resting on the floor, the curved shape of the drawers lends a soothing, organic feel to a workroom. **A curtain rod mounted on a desktop**, *below left*, turns a roll of paper into an inexhaustible blotter or inspirational sketchpad. **A craft table fitted with compartments and covered in Perspex**, *above*, is perfect for someone who likes to keep supplies – say, for beadwork or jewellery design – in plain sight, while accenting the desktop with colour.

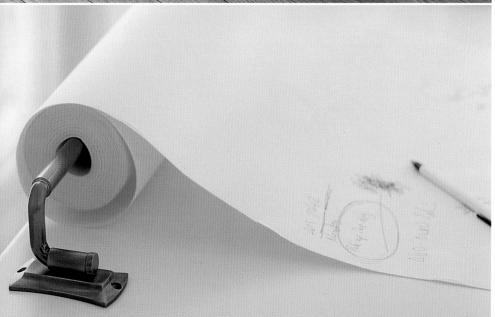

The Adventures

The Memoirs

lighting

The Casr-Book

His Last Bow

Lighting is a crucial component in the design of any room. A successful lighting plan not only banishes darkness but also creates mood, defines the overall space, and accentuates different zones within it. For an office, lighting plays an important functional role as well, illuminating work areas for optimum clarity while helping to prevent eye fatigue.

Many of us have little or no control over the lighting we work by at our jobs. Yet the way a room is lit has been proven to affect health and productivity, beginning with the quality of primary purpose, such as a bedroom or living room, something as simple as a pair of sconces or pendant lamps on either side of a desk help designate the area as a work zone. A careful plan for ambient lighting, one that illuminates each station, can make the subdivision of a space appear more graceful and less of an afterthought.

Task lighting is exactly what the name describes – and more. It's focussed, flexible, and generally brighter than ambient lighting. Task lights can take the form of traditional desk lamps, overhead track lighting, recessed spots, halogen

Light, both natural and artificial, is what brings a workspace to life. Combine task and ambient lighting to provide flexibility and add a measure of warmth.

its ambient (or overall atmospheric) lighting. Whether your workspace is used mainly during daylight hours or exclusively in the evenings, ensure that the lighting is bright enough to illuminate all areas of the room. If your office is quite large, install a dimmer system to make the lighting plan more flexible. This will allow you to tone down the light in lesser-used areas of the room and cut down on the electricity bill as well.

In a high-ceilinged workroom, suspend a row of pendant lights low enough to concentrate light where it is most needed, and to create a more intimate overall atmosphere. When a home office shares space in a room with a different swing-arm lamps, or any combination thereof. Task lights are usually the most versatile part of a workroom's lighting plan in both practical and aesthetic terms. Necessary and decorative, task lights can easily be moved to accommodate the work being done, while their style and their effect on the feeling of a space can be quickly and simply altered with a change of shade or bulb wattage. Adjustable desk lamps are often the most accommodating options because they can be positioned to suit a variety of work tasks.

Like candlelight in a dining room, the lights you choose to write or sketch by instantly add warmth and character to a workspace.

The Right Light, Day or Night

In a large and sunny home office, a flexible lighting plan makes the most of sunlight while helping cut down on glare. Adjustable window treatments, combined with well-placed task lighting and accent lamps, offer illumination when and where you need it.

Who wouldn't welcome a workroom blessed with natural light and views of the outdoors? But even the most enviably sun-drenched office poses lighting challenges. How do you control glare by day and light the space after dark? The solution for this poolside office has three parts: versatile task and accent lighting, adjustable window treatments to help tame sunlight, and an all-white palette that makes the most of both bright sunlight and soft illumination.

Window treatments are especially important if your desk is positioned in front of a window. Canvas roller blinds in white provide just the right light filter. Easily adjusted to the height of the sun at different times of day, they successfully reduce glare while admitting plenty of ambient light and providing an unimpeded view of the outdoors. Sheer curtains in a pale colour are another practical way to diffuse strong sunlight while maintaining a bright, airy atmosphere.

A variety of lighting types allows an easy transition from daytime to evening illumination. Versatile swing-arm lamps, fitted with halogen bulbs and fabric shades, offer clear white task lighting, while discreetly placed gallery lights cast a soft incandescent glow throughout the room.

Roller blinds, *left*, adjust easily to filter the constant play of light throughout the day. **Halogen task lamps**, *right*, and small lamps nestled between books on the shelves, offer a range of lighting options when darkness falls.

With natural light flooding in from three sides, a bright office benefits from streamlined white furnishings and accessories in soft shades of blue. A simple colour scheme unifies a workspace that serves many purposes. Once you've set up a neutral canvas, create zones that will keep piles of work from interfering with leisure time. A light-reflective palette connects the different zones and emphasizes the spaciousness of the room.

An adjustable lamp with vellum shade, *above*, can swing into action as either a desk lamp or reading light. A built-in high-backed sofa, *right*, offers ample resting space for family and visitors while helping to define the office space behind it. Plenty of storage – on shelves and in drawers tucked into the framework of the sofa – helps eliminate the clutter of office supplies.

In the evening, soft pools of light dramatically redefine this room's contours, carving out several zones for work or relaxation. A variety of lighting – direct and indirect, halogen and incandescent – works in tandem to highlight architectural details, create mood, and provide clear, focussed light for reading or other close work. A system of switches and dimmers makes it simple to control the room's many light fixtures from the entrance.

Night falls, and, like a stage set, a home office is transformed by lighting.

Simple but stylish gallery lights are aimed in two different directions: upwards, to bathe the walls in a pale wash of light, and downwards, as accent lighting, to illuminate artwork. Articulated task lamps behind the sofa and at the computer can be easily adjusted as needed, making them an especially versatile choice for a multi-use room. Hidden under-shelf lighting offers both sides of the desktop a clear task light, leaving the surface free as a work area.

Gallery lights turned towards the ceiling, *left*, accentuate the loftiness of the room and highlight the dedicated work area. **When aimed downwards**, *right*, the dimmable halogen lights wash artwork and white walls with a warm glow.

Design Details

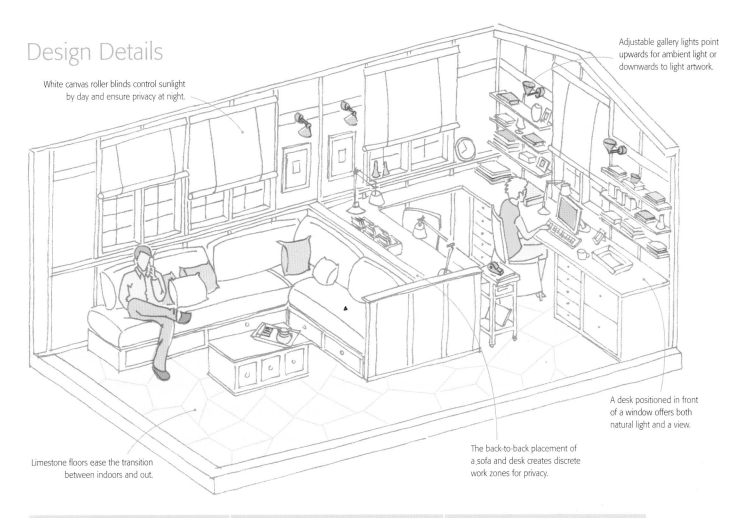

White canvas roller blinds control sunlight by day and ensure privacy at night.

Adjustable gallery lights point upwards for ambient light or downwards to light artwork.

A desk positioned in front of a window offers both natural light and a view.

The back-to-back placement of a sofa and desk creates discrete work zones for privacy.

Limestone floors ease the transition between indoors and out.

Colour Palette

A palette of blue and white, with a few well-placed blue-green accents, is at one with the natural setting of this sunny poolside office – but could make any workroom feel nearer the water. The all-white treatment of walls, windows, and furniture is a perfect foil for the decorative notes of blue and blue-green that dot the room, from a graduated set of funnels arranged on a window sill to storage boxes tucked beneath a shelf.

Room Plan

Back-to-back work and leisure zones make the most of this shared space, providing each with a sense of privacy and a clearly defined central focus. The dedicated work area is arranged along a windowed wall, with supplies and files placed within easy reach on shelves above the desk or on a table behind it. A high-backed sofa lined up with the worktable (the built-in structure here could be easily replicated with a standard high-backed sofa and a free-standing table) both defines the relaxation zone and serves as a divider.

Materials

Cotton canvas A strong fabric that holds its shape, cotton canvas softens through repeated washings, and can be dressed up with accessories or kept casual.

Ticking A tightly woven fabric classic, cotton ticking comes in a variety of striped patterns. Use it for cushions, loose covers, or blinds.

Limestone One of the softest natural stones, limestone is quarried from evaporated sea and lake beds, and ages beautifully.

The Night Shift

Arrange a comfortable corner office for night-time and weekend use. Provide adjustable levels of light to give after-hours workers a range of options, from functional task lighting to a cosy glow.

Transform the simplest of corner desk arrangements into an inviting office with a flexible lighting plan to accommodate all tasks at hand. This office combines three basic types of lighting for an intimate, layered effect: task lighting at the desk, ambient lighting on the side table, and a unique accent light on the overhead shelf. Dimmers adjust brightness for reading or computer work.

A shapely table lamp, *left*, defines the corner nook with a glow of soft light. **An adjustable desk lamp**, *above*, is ideal for close reading and paperwork. **An accent light on an upper shelf**, *right*, helps to banish shadows.

Ambient

Ambient lighting is the main illumination in a room, the background light that gives a space a warm and welcoming atmosphere. Ambient light often has multiple sources, which can include natural sunlight, ceiling-hung fixtures, floor lamps, and track lights. A combination of window blinds and artificial lighting allows you to adjust the amount of light in a room. For a warm, flattering light, use incandescent bulbs in translucent glass fixtures. Avoid fluorescent bulbs for overhead fixtures, and install dimmers for ease in adjusting light throughout the day.

Suspended globe light

Task

Task lighting is focussed lighting. It's meant to illuminate a specific work area, a designated part of a room, the papers on your desk, or the chair you sit in to read. In a large room, you will probably need several task lights. They can be large or small, fixed or movable, but all should have shades that direct light cleanly onto the areas needing illumination. As a rule, incandescent bulbs cast the softest light, halogen the brightest and most focussed. Metal shades are best for directing light but they can also conduct heat, so be careful where you place them.

Articulated desk lamp

Accent

Accent lights are the decorative notes in a room. They are optional in the sense that they are not strictly necessary to the room's purpose, yet they're essential for how they subtly add a measure of beauty and drama to a room's decor. Accent lights draw attention to paintings and objects and deftly accentuate architectural details. Standing alone, they can light up a dark corner and make a room appear larger and more welcoming. In an office, accent lights can help demarcate different work or activity zones without being too obvious.

Cage light

ambient, task, and accent lighting for your workspace

Pendant lights

Recessed downlights

Track lights

Suspended globe lights cast a diffused glow throughout a room and are an effective source of ambient light.

Pendant lights cast wide beams of light over work areas and help light up corners.

Recessed downlights are discrete, yet deliver lots of diffuse light to a room.

Track lights can be adjusted to bounce light off a ceiling or wall, or provide it directly.

Swing-arm floor lamp

Under-shelf light

Sconce light

Articulated desk lamps with adjustable arms and heads direct light where you need it.

Swing-arm floor lamps are a versatile choice. When not in use for reading, they can add welcome ambient light.

Under-shelf lights provide space-saving, focussed illumination for a workstation.

Sconce lights are a practical solution when desktop surface space is at a premium.

Table lamp

Picture light

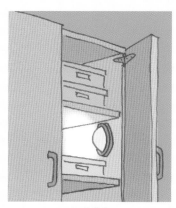

Touch light

Cage lights are no-nonsense accents that are both practical and economical for utility rooms and other work areas.

Table lamps come in a variety of styles and easily add light to a desktop or bookshelf.

Picture lights cast direct soft light onto photographs, paintings, bulletin boards, or collections.

Touch lights are motion- or touch-activated, making them ideal for drawers and cupboards.

organizing

Getting organized not only results in a cleaner, neater workspace, it also turns out to be its own best reward. A well-organized workroom means fewer lost files and fewer mislaid tools, but it can also contribute much to the harmony of our everyday lives. Knowing how to organize a workroom is even a useful life skill that you can pass on to your children: a couple of shoeboxes and a felt-tip pen make a perfect starter kit.

The first step in bringing order to a room is in some ways the easiest, but it's often the most

different items: divide tax records by year; garden tools by long-handled versus short; arts and crafts supplies into paper, paint, and sticky things; and sort family photographs into trips, graduations, weddings, and birthdays. Make this process of subdividing by categories your starting point, and you'll never be overwhelmed when confronted with a pile of stuff in need of a system.

The next step is to store what you've kept and organize it with an eye towards access. Things you use every day belong where you can easily reach them – at eye-level on open shelving, in desk

Whether it's your own private writing retreat or a shared home office, a well-organized workspace helps make you more productive and keeps things calm.

avoided: paring down. The sooner you get rid of what you no longer need, the sooner you can get down to organizing what you want to keep. You'll not only feel as if you're travelling lighter, you'll have a much smaller job to finish. Focus on one corner at a time, getting rid of outdated files, computer disks you no longer need, rusted tools, articles you will never read, or obsolete office supplies. Make a sweep of your bookshelves and magazine racks, and pack up the extras to deliver to your local charity shop.

Take a good look at what remains, and divide everything into categories that make sense to you. This approach works equally well for a variety of

drawers, or in a filing cabinet. Less frequently used items can be stored on high shelves or in another room altogether. The point of organization is not to banish items, but to know how to put your hands on them when you need them.

The systems you devise to stash what you've sorted will naturally differ from one workroom to another – a pegboard makes less sense for an accountant's office than it does for an architect's draughting space – but the same general principles apply. Store small items like paper clips, rubber bands, and tacks in small containers, keep like with like, label things clearly, and then sit back and enjoy the calm of your orderly office.

Outfitting a Workshop

A compact workshop offers ideas for organization and display that any handy person would do well to borrow. Its clearly defined work areas – and clever combination of everyday and antique tools stored in plain sight – make a place for everything, and keep everything in place.

For anyone who is handy, the appeal of woodworking, boatbuilding, sewing, or crafting is not only the end product but also the pure pleasure of the tools involved. In every home, tools are basic, beautiful, and essential. Whether modern gadgets or collected antique hand tools, the storage of these items is as much about keeping them carefully organized as it is about showing them to their best advantage. A kitchen drawer won't do, nor will a jumbled shelf in the garage. Frequently used tools need to be easy to find and within reach of your main workspace. A prized collection, whether it's antique tools, a child's artwork, or favourite examples of your handiwork, should be proudly displayed as a source of inspiration.

When creating a workshop with room for both storage and display, make the most of the space at hand. Cover walls with pegboard for mounting tools. Employ shallow boxes or trays to subdivide work surfaces and clear space quickly. This workroom is a good example. Simple and efficiently designed, the empty space under the worktop is maximized, and separate areas of the room are designated specifically for drawing and paperwork.

A collection of antique planes, bevels, and brushes, *left*, is hung on pegboard alongside everyday tools in a handsome combination of storage and display. Trays made from wood samples and standard drawer pulls can be set aside when more space is needed. A specially cut pegboard, *right*, is painted blue to give the space energy and show off the shapely tools.

This highly functional workshop makes the most of every inch of space with zones for drawing, woodworking, and paperwork. Everything needed at each station is well within reach, and traffic flows easily among all areas. For maximum flexibility, a long worktop with storage underneath provides extra room; projects and supplies are stowed in baskets below. The industrial appearance of a sturdy rubber mat belies its comfort for standing jobs; it also serves as a debris catcher to protect the wooden floor.

A tension rod mounted between the eaves, *above*, is a clever mix of form and function. Fitted with inexpensive boat hooks to hang tools and illustrations, the system is easily adapted to other kinds of utility spaces or workrooms. **The long worktop**, *right*, runs the length of the room, where it meets the office nook. A simple slab top of cheap timber and rough-framed cubbyholes in varying sizes make it easy to locate stored materials.

To further define each area, include seating suited to the task – a tall stool pulled up to the drawing board, a school-style desk chair in the office nook, an adjustable ergonomic chair at the computer workstation. In this versatile space, the three distinct work zones are visually connected by the colour palette and a repetition of gently worn wood.

In a well-planned office, everything you need to finish your project is exactly where you left it.

You'll want to keep essential tools close at hand to stay organized. Here, this principle is executed within a discrete space for drawing tucked under the eaves. You can make the most of an unconventional space with the help of spring clamps that pin drawing tools to the rafters and papers to the desktop. The versatile drawing board is suited to work done standing or perched on a stool. For focussed task lighting, use a swing-arm lamp clamped to a table for close work, leaving the desk surface free for drawing materials, elbows, and coffee.

Industrial spring clamps, *left*, put necessities on display and add to the room's purposeful look. **An under-the-eaves nook**, *right*, is kept clear, with drawings stored underneath and nearby.

Colour Palette

Like the earth and sky, brown and blue make a natural pair. Walls painted petrol blue and a sloping ceiling brightened by a wash of white paint add old-fashioned charm to a woodworker's studio that boasts as many shades of brown as a forest. Casually mismatched wood samples, in a variety of types from ash to mahogany, set the tone for shades of brown to repeat throughout the room. The resulting palette is as soothing to the soul as the work that gets done in the room.

It's possible to carve an efficient office area out of a potentially "lost" space: a chest for organizing paperwork fits nicely into the eaves beneath a sloping ceiling. Fitted with a low filing cabinet and a sliding keyboard tray, this corner desk makes the most of its low-profile space, and offers all that's needed for paperwork and filing tasks. With supplies for book-keeping and a space for doing research, this cosy attic corner becomes an out-of-the-way station for keeping track of current projects and new ideas.

Materials

Redwood A reddish brown softwood, redwood is known for its strength, the ease with which it is worked, and its resistance to decay and ability to withstand harsh weather conditions.

Pegboard The humble pegboard may be the smartest storage system ever devised: a sheet of perforated composite board cut to size and mounted where you want it. Pegs or hooks inserted into the holes hold tools and supplies.

Anti-fatigue matting A good investment in a workroom where you spend a lot of time on your feet, anti-fatigue matting is designed to ease pressure on joints. Originally created for commercial use, it comes in a variety of thicknesses, colours, and materials. Most have a rubber base and will hold up through years of use.

The office area, *left*, is arranged for ease of use with an L-shaped desk that combines a computer workspace and a filing centre in one compact corner. **Wooden trays with handles**, *above*, offer portable storage for samples and equipment.

Easy-to-See Storage

A family office relies on a clever labelling and storage system for supplies. Put an eye-catching picture or bold colour on it, give it a designated location, and it will be there when you need it.

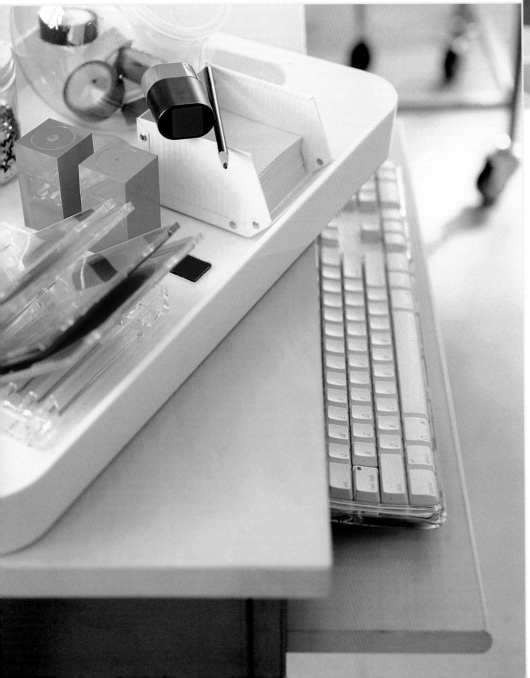

Maintaining family office storage is easy once you've got a system in place. Create an office supplies library – an all-in-one unit that concentrates storage in a single area and leaves the rest of the space free for projects. Arrange contents in clear containers or give them colourful labels for easy recognition. Store small items like paper clips or tacks in clear jars; mark tins holding tape and other necessities with colour copies of the contents for easy spotting. Group all containers by type and size for a neat appearance.

A portable white tray, *left*, is an all-in-one desktop tray. Colour-coded Velcro tabs signal placement of supplies and keep them in position for transport. **Images of contents**, *above*, make colourful labels for storage. **A wall of open shelving**, *right*, makes it easy to see just what you need at a glance.

Recycled containers used in multiples, *above*, make a strong visual statement, and can be individually labelled for storage. Tea caddies, coffee tins, and other vessels with reusable lids are a natural home for hardware. **Colour-coded tags**, *above right*, can be used to differentiate closed containers by family member or season. Vintage trunks are an especially attractive choice for storage kept out in the open. **Salvaged accessories**, *right*, such as a dish rack turned letter rack, often make the best containers and add a touch of wit to a desktop or worktop.

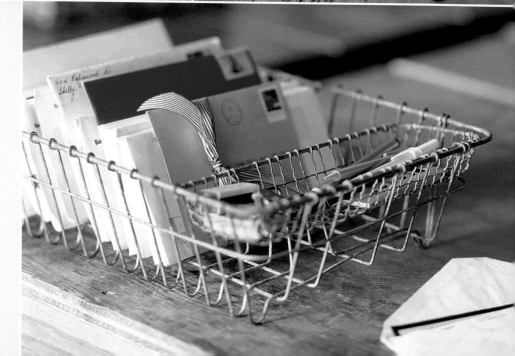

How to Organize Office Supplies

Being able to put your hands on the right tool or the right file when you need it is the goal of any organizing system. Whether it's hardware, tax records, or family photos, the same basic rules apply: edit, separate, categorize, label, and file. While you're at it, find unusual accessories to use as personal organizers. Browse flea markets and car boot sales for containers with built-in dividers; post-office sorting bins, apothecary cabinets, and toast racks are all organizing naturals. Keep tags and permanent markers on hand for labelling closed storage, and plenty of compact containers at the ready for keeping track of small items.

A construction worker's tool bag, *left*, makes an amusing portable office for anyone whose work involves meeting with clients on site; filled with tools, it would make an equally useful home-repair kit. Small items, *above*, are best stored in small spaces, like this wooden craft-supplies holder, attractive enough to display on a desktop. Keeping loose everyday items like rubber bands and paper clips in their own compartments means never having to sort through a junk drawer.

storage

In a dedicated workroom that must be kept organized and look orderly at the end of the day, smart storage is a plus. But if a workspace has multiple uses – whether it doubles as a guest room, occupies a corner of the living room, or takes over a nook in the kitchen – a thoughtfully designed storage system is indispensable.

Before choosing your office storage, make an inventory of your workroom, equipment, and supplies, and take a good look at the possibilities of the space at hand. Take stock of items that should be left out for daily use (pens and pencils, are paper documents and business records, an investment in the most attractive filing cabinet or filing boxes you can afford makes the most sense. Be creative. If a polished wooden finish is not your style, employ a distressed bookshelf outfitted with baskets or a traditional two-drawer steel filing cabinet. If your workspace has height, install shelving that reaches to the ceiling, complete with a library ladder to access the highest shelf.

Above all, storage should perform double duty in a workroom. A stool with a removable lid can be used for extra seating as well as spare storage

Smart storage eliminates clutter and clears the way for a calm and creative workday. Simplify your home office with storage solutions that fit the way you work.

computer, calendar, filing baskets, supplies). Then look at the things that need to be filed or shelved for easy access (current work, reference articles, samples, paint pots), and what can be stashed in long-term storage (completed jobs, tax records, photo negatives, report cards, user manuals). Once you've established what goes in which category, you're almost there.

How best to organize storage depends on what needs to be put away. Open shelves make ideal storage for books, large craft supplies, containers filled with smaller items like paper clips or rubber bands, or baskets filled with stationery, magazines, or CDs. If your workroom's main products in an office that shares space with a den. A filing cabinet can be topped with a vase of flowers and a lamp to stand in for a guest-room bedside table.

When space in a workroom is limited, find a place for the overflow in an adjacent hallway, or install a shelf overhead to add architectural detailing as well as extra storage. If you prefer the look of a tidy office over a filled-to-capacity desk, or if your office shares space with another area, relegate most items to a roll-top desk or a wardrobe so you can close the doors on your supplies. The point of workroom storage, after all, is not simply the area it takes up, but the space that's left free and clear for work.

Options for an Organized Office

Open storage in a professional home office not only inspires order, but also offers rich returns in flexibility, access, and visual impact. Make a virtue of necessity by integrating storage with display, and use built-in storage to define discrete zones in a workspace.

The most successful office storage systems address every type, size, and shape of storage a space requires. They also cater to the nature of a workspace, and its inhabitants. You don't need to be a psychologist to know what stimulates the creative process, whether in a nursery classroom or a graphic design office: variety, colour, shape, pattern, order. Nothing facilitates that kind of mix – or is as likely to improve on a room's original bones – as simply as built-in shelving. Built-in shelves provide an organizing framework, visually and practically. They make ideal room dividers, literally – when used to separate a reception area from a dedicated work zone, or a home office from the rest of the house – as well as visually, defining one part of the room as a dedicated storage and display area.

Here, striking floor-to-ceiling built-in shelves delineate the principal workspace and help define a pair of inviting reading nooks. Mounted on an industrial track, one unit glides noiselessly open and shut with the pull of a handle for easy access to (or quick concealment of) an adjacent master bedroom. Custom made of warm wood to integrate with the rest of the house, the shelving units have a pleasing, one-of-a-kind look that makes them a decorative element as well.

A sliding storage wall, *left*, provides generous storage for both active and archival files, with plenty of room left for display. **Custom-cut sheets of galvanized metal**, *right*, make sleek magnetic clipboards when fitted to shelves, and are within easy reach of the desk when the wall slides shut.

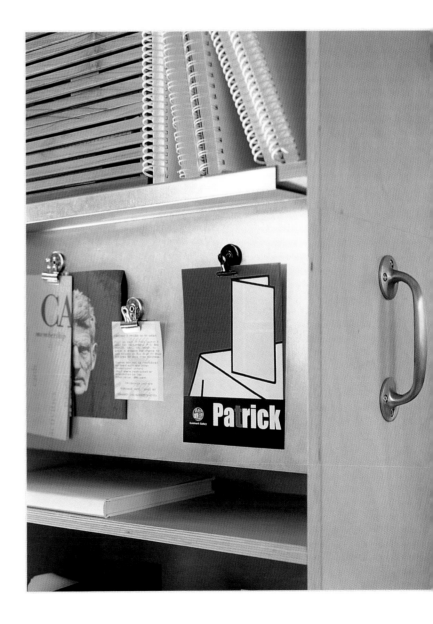

When organizing shelves, place active files – those you use every day – at eye-level, reserving the highest and lowest shelves for office archives and other materials you use less often. For a more orderly appearance, organize by type and style of storage. Arrange bound folders on adjacent shelves, reference books in a single row, and small items in matching containers. When clutter is unavoidable, screen shelves with a photograph or pinboard cut to fit.

A graceful desktop composition, *above*, picks up on the shapes and colours of the surrounding space. **The half-open storage wall**, *right*, reveals its role as a room divider and its versatility as a storage unit. The wall slides closed to further define the desk area and bring supplies within easy reach. Each of the deep shelves is used to the fullest for files or reference materials.

One of the advantages of built-in storage is the way it can be used to fill in or even reconfigure awkward spaces. In this home office, the twin shelving units not only turn the walls into useful storage space, they also create the illusion of extra room by extending the office area into the hallway. Handsome and sleek from every angle, the built-in units camouflage a narrow hallway and make the layout seem enviably spacious.

In a home office, flexible storage offers more than just versatility. It gives you the freedom to work anywhere you want.

A flexible display system with a hanging shelf makes a corner alcove into a welcoming place to relax or receive clients, away from the confines of the desk. A chrome drinks trolley is pressed into library service in this narrow space. With the help of the bookshelf wall, the two office zones are effortlessly linked, inviting use of every part of the space.

A sunny reading corner, *left*, makes a welcoming way station for reviewing files or consulting a book from the shelves that line the adjacent wall. **A chrome drinks trolley**, *right*, makes unexpected but useful library storage.

Design Details

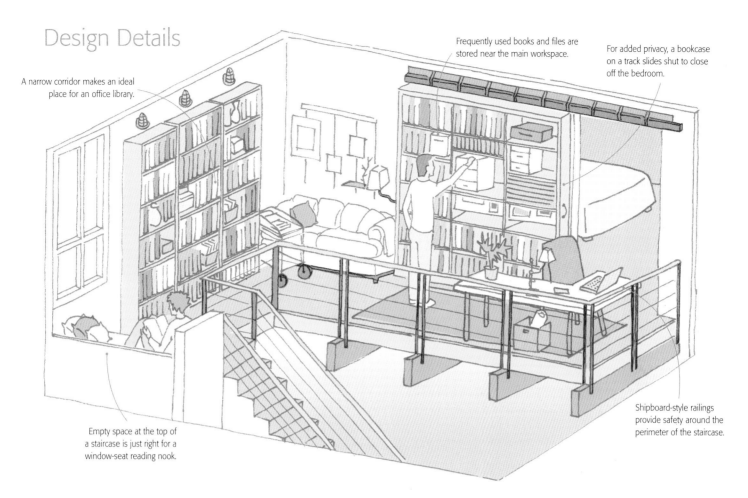

A narrow corridor makes an ideal place for an office library.

Frequently used books and files are stored near the main workspace.

For added privacy, a bookcase on a track slides shut to close off the bedroom.

Empty space at the top of a staircase is just right for a window-seat reading nook.

Shipboard-style railings provide safety around the perimeter of the staircase.

Colour Palette

Bold spaces invite bold colour but they don't need to broadcast it. In a winning combination that mixes subtlety and brilliance, the creamy walls and blond wood of this modern office's flooring, shelves, and railings are enlivened with several splashes of bright red, in small and large doses. Black provides sleek punctuation, and the overall effect is harmonious and handsome. Colour is an energetic element of the whole.

Room Plan

Style meets practicality in a multi-zoned office that makes ingenious use of the narrow leftover space of a wraparound stairwell hallway. By necessity, each element of this workspace occupies its own sliver of space, but the overall composition creates an ideal home office. Combined to striking visual and practical effect are: a private desk with a view of its own and easy access to an adjacent bedroom and bathroom; a double expanse of shelving and storage space; and two distinct seating areas that invite both working and relaxing.

Materials

Leather Made from tanned animal hides, leather is one of nature's most durable and flexible materials. It's a good choice for upholstery.

Glass Plate glass used as a desktop or table top adds a welcome note of lightness to a workroom. It can also be used as an overlay on a wooden desktop.

Natural wood For built-in or free-standing shelves, a high-grade pine or hardwood will prevent sagging and add a touch of warmth to an office.

Room for Work and Play

An efficient office is one thing, a creative space for children is another. How do you design a shared workspace that welcomes users big and small? Place storage at every level, then add witty accents.

With a little imagination and plenty of well-planned storage, even the busiest home office can be made into an organized room for family projects. A built-in desk and a spacious work-table allow access from all sides and at every level. Keep clutter at bay with numbered boxes and storage bins assigned to each family member.

Count on numbering, *left*, to keep supplies sorted out: label boxes with house numbers for a ready-made storage system. **Paint-mixing cups**, *above*, store office supplies so they are within reach and easy to share. **A roll of drawing paper**, *right*, is fixed to the desk with a curtain rod. Storage and seating at many levels accommodate family members of all sizes.

milo   ella   nina

How to Make Storage Unique

Sometimes the perfect container for what you need to store today was once the perfect container for something else. Now it's empty and just waiting to be put back into action. Car boot sales and second-hand shops are great sources for unique storage solutions, but chances are you've got a collection of alternative containers waiting to be discovered the next time you clean out the garage, sort through a kitchen cupboard, or get organized for a car boot sale of your own. Whether it's your grandfather's old toolbox, a revolving spice rack, or a favourite set of nesting bowls, many practical items can be put to work as creative office storage.

A **weathered metal postbox**, *above*, paired with a wire-basket in-tray makes a whimsical and a hard-to-overlook reminder to post the monthly bills. **A 1930s straw dispenser**, *above right*, was borrowed from a milk bar and converted into a pencil holder for a craft room. **The deep drawer of a truckle bed**, *right*, can be fitted with one or more hanging file frames to stand in for the family filing cabinet and still leave room for pillows and extra bedding.

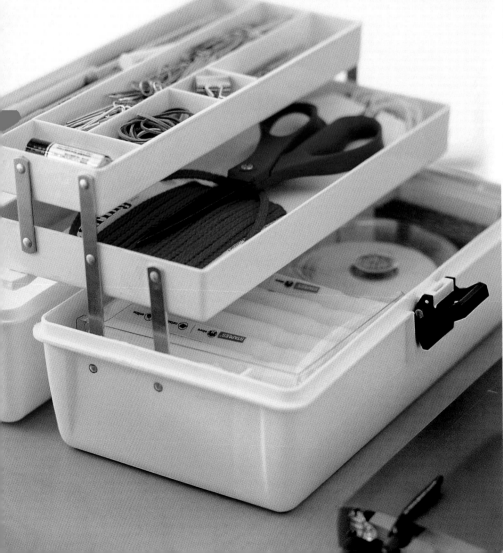

A folding carpenter's ruler, *above*, set flat
on a desktop, makes a practical business card
holder, photo gallery, or deadline reminder.
The same system works for recipe cards in the
kitchen or even for incoming post. A multi-tiered
plastic tackle box, *left*, is an especially versatile
container. Use it to organize office supplies,
to store costume jewellery (or jewellery-making
supplies), as a sewing or crafts kit, or even as
a lightweight tool kit. Decorated with coloured
stickers and a child's name or initials, it would
make an irresistible treasure chest. Pick up a
few tackle boxes to keep in each cupboard and
see if they don't do the trick for storing those
little easy-to-lose items that accumulate in
almost every room of the house.

accessories

The idea that hard work requires a simplified setting is a myth. In fact, the opposite is true. A workspace furnished with beautiful things is an inspiration. It not only provides a welcoming place in which to do your best work, but it also helps to stimulate creativity. After the desk is in place and it's time to add accessories to a workroom, the best advice is to follow your heart and your aesthetic instincts.

When it comes to accessorizing your work area, the line between useful and decorative is easily blurred. Many accessories make the "useful" but a revolving spice rack or a well-worn vintage bottle crate can also organize a desktop while adding personality and style.

Keep an open mind as you look for new ways to turn well-loved objects into office accessories. Instead of standard plastic in- and out-trays, try a few handsome canvas bins or a pair of brightly coloured lacquer serving trays. Make a desktop file from a vintage silver toast rack or a magnetic bulletin board from a salvaged metal sign. Turn a chrome drinks trolley into a library trolley to keep books or works-in-progress close at hand.

Traditional office supplies might do the trick. But, employing well-loved antiques and recycling objects as desk accessories adds wit and style to your desktop.

category with ease: a telephone, a desk lamp, a wastebasket, a stapler, and a tape dispenser. Quite a few "extras" will seem indispensable to some but less important to others: a coffeemaker, a thick rug, a colourful cushion to ease back strain.

Think of accessories as your friendly support staff, the assistants that keep your papers in order and your tools at hand, protect your desktop or the floor underneath, store your stationery, and keep your books neatly arranged. Fortunes have been made designing containers and systems for all these purposes, but there's also a wealth of stylish alternatives to be found in unexpected objects. Traditional office supplies can do the job,

Workspace accessories should energize and amuse you throughout the workday. They should also be easy to use and well suited to their tasks. Pick and choose among your own store of treasures first, and you may find practical objects that fill your office with humour and delight. If the lamp that saw you through university still feels lucky, dust it off and put it on proud display. Fashion a bookshelf from a favourite garden bench, a small bulletin board from an heirloom picture frame, a notepaper holder from an empty cigar box. It's these personal details that bring life and style to your home office or workspace and make it a pleasure to get down to business.

A Working Holiday

Weekend workspaces offer refuge from the demands of daily life,
along with all the equipment it requires. When furnishing an office
in a holiday retreat, forgo fast-track efficiency and surround yourself
with inspirational mementos and comfortable things you love.

Weekend homes have a way of breaking rules and bending definitions. They reflect a looser, more comfortable style based in casual furnishings and quirky collections. Memories are made in summer homes, a fact their comfortable, well-loved furnishings and eclectic displays reflect. If you long for an office with the same relaxed getaway atmosphere, it makes sense to furnish it with favourite objects given a new life: a wicker rocking chair brought in from the veranda, a garden bench recycled as a bookshelf. Let sentiment play a role in deciding which furnishings merit this new approach to the office. Imagination and a willingness to experiment are what make it all work together.

Accessories easily bridge the gap between the traditional home-office and holiday-home style. Outfit a standard worktable with seashells to hold paper clips and drawing pins; put a tea towel on the desk to stand in for a blotter. Accessories add grace to a room. Something as simple as a set of matching cushions can transform a pair of mismatched seats into a harmonious couple. Creative groupings of accessories on a desktop or a window sill can redefine the style of an office with minimal effort.

A farmhouse-style table, *left*, dressed with a cotton tea towel and an old wire dish drainer for filing post, makes an informal weekend work surface. **Silver-plated heirlooms**, *right*, and a wooden cutlery tray make practical desk accessories and beautiful containers for office supplies.

An all-season veranda converted into an office is an ideal place to put souvenirs to work. A soft palette of blue and white is reinforced by simple accessories that bring nature into every corner of the room. Labelled starfish on the walls conjure a history of family beachcombing. Clear glass lamps and a rug add comfort and bolster the casual mood. Pieces that earned their nicks serving generations blend with more recent acquisitions to produce a timeless look.

Messages in bottles, *above*, decorate a window ledge, reinforcing the seaside theme. **Benches painted in cool beach tones**, *right*, turn leftover space under windows into a useful storage area for books, magazines, and writing supplies. A pile of cushions turns a bench into an impromptu window seat. Woven baskets add a second tier of flexible storage underneath and make for quick tidying-up when company is expected.

Even a weekend workspace needs to be flexible, especially if it's shared by a family. A bulletin board and a few work surfaces are basic necessities. Here, a simple painted table anchors a command centre for jotting down messages, writing postcards, and checking appointments. And, though we'd like to forget them, the demands of everyday life follow us on holiday: an old clock face that dominates a carefully composed still life humorously keeps track of where your family needs to be and when.

In a holiday workroom, accessories help preserve precious memories of weekends past.

The simple beauty of handwritten letters, objects found in nature, and beloved souvenirs takes precedence over modern electronics. In place of a filing cabinet or office sideboard that might intrude upon this serene setting, woven baskets arranged on the table's lower shelf store post, magazines, and newspapers.

A painted Victorian table, *left*, has been refinished to serve as a country-style desk. A supply of stick-on notes turns a clock face into an appointment calendar. **A pinboard made from a simple wooden frame**, *right*, blends in with the room's soft palette.

Colour Palette

Blue, white, and taupe come together for a classic seaside palette and are the perfect colour combination for conjuring memories of relaxed days on the beach. Taking its cue from the view outside the windows, the natural rug in this office extends over the unfinished wood floor like a blanket on the sand. Blue-painted panelling wraps the room in a watery hue. Creamy white trim and a few furnishings painted blue-green add clean, crisp accents to the soothing, simple palette.

Materials

Panelling A traditional wood cladding for walls in older houses, panelling may cover only the lower portion of a room, marked by a decorative chair rail, or extend the full height of a room.

Painted wood Paint seals wood and creates a smooth surface that is easy to clean. Speciality paints, such as milk paints and crackle glazes, produce an appealing weathered look that complements vintage furnishings. Unfinished pine is a natural for painting, and takes well to both glossy finishes and more traditional ones.

Wicker Made by tightly weaving supple willow branches or lengths of rattan around a sturdy frame, wicker is used to make graceful baskets and furnishings. Though less durable than wood, wicker can last a century or more.

Muted shades of blue form a backdrop to a charming variety of benches and children's stools that displays a family's well-worn collection of summer-home reading. Stacking low tables and stools against a wall is an easy way to invent extra storage that doubles as seating when needed. A gently weathered rocking chair is a must for creating a contemplative corner in a holiday home. The honey tones of the floorboards and the softness of the jute rug make this spot a natural draw for rainy-day readers.

A reclaimed architectural detail, *left*, becomes a clever porthole-shaped letter file. Instead of being relegated to the attic, a well-used wooden tricycle acts as transport for books. **A family's love of found starfish**, *above*, creates a thematic wall display.

Kitchen Office Classics

A tidy, compact office is a bonus for any kitchen.
To integrate work and cooking areas, make use
of your favourite kitchen tools as witty office
accessories to organize your workspace.

A kitchen is a perfect location for
an office nook – a space to jot down
a note to a friend, make lists for a
party, or pay the monthly bills while
finishing a cup of coffee. Pair a small
workspace with flexible, recycled
storage. Alternative uses of kitchen
tools create a stylish, integrated look:
a wire whisk doubles as a business
card holder, a glass biscuit jar stores
office necessities, a magnetic spice
rack holds small office supplies.

A chrome bread bin, *left*, plays stationery supply
station while a measuring cup holds necessities.
A spice rack and straw holders, *above*, make
new homes for paper clips and pens. **A lazy
Susan on a shelf**, *right*, serves up office supplies.

Office Ergonomics

However visually appealing your workspace, the hours you spend there will be enjoyable only as long as you're comfortable. Finding the right combination of chair, desk, lighting, and computer positions requires some experimentation. Still, a few general principles apply, whatever your set-up. First, determine how you can arrange your workstation to prevent stress-related discomfort in the back, shoulders, and wrists. Work chairs should be adjustable by height, and those with armrests should be positioned low enough to permit your shoulders to relax. Feet should rest comfortably on the floor. Position task lighting so it shines neither in your eyes nor directly on the computer screen. Your computer keyboard and mouse should be set at a 100-degree angle from your torso, to allow you to type and control the mouse without bending your wrists unnaturally. Place your computer screen directly in front of you at eye-level, in order to prevent neck strain.

A desk for bill paying, *opposite*, combines plenty of writing surface with divided storage compartments placed within easy reach and at eye-level.

Organized principally for telephone work, *above right*, this desk divides surface space by function. A speakerphone and a stand for documents both help prevent neck strain. To use a laptop on your desk, prop it up on a stack of books until it sits at eye-level.

A computer station, *right*, employs a keyboard tray to reduce wrist strain and back fatigue. If you work for extended periods at the computer, it's well worth investing in an ergonomically designed desk chair or using a lumbar pillow for lower back support and a foot stool to help prevent hip strain.

How to Create a Custom Calendar

Diaries and organizers make fine Mother's and Father's Day gifts, but the everyday life of a busy family demands a family calendar – big, bold, and impossible to overlook. Put it where everyone in your home is sure to see it, and make it a showstopper: devote an entire wall to keeping the chores and appointments of the month straight. Measure the available wall space, divide by the number of heads in your household, and proceed with one of these four solutions to transform a standard frame, blackboard, whiteboard, or corkboard into an eye-catching organizational system.

Day-of-the-week corkboard strips, *above*, let you track everyone's comings and goings, and post telephone messages, reminders, and even small easy-to-lose items like car keys.
A framed Perspex grid, *right*, makes an easily annotated perpetual calendar. Each day of the month gets its own roomy square, and each member of the family has his or her own coloured marker to note appointments and leave messages. The wipe-off surface allows you to start fresh every month.

An oversize magnetic blackboard, *left*, reinvents the message board. Mount it in the hall or over the kitchen table. Scribble in the week's dentist appointments and football matches, post invitations and reminders, and persuade your family to do the same. Stick to pure black and white for a sleek, graphic look, or use coloured chalk and bright magnets to personalize messages and timetables. A framed whiteboard, *above*, fitted with hooks for keys, erasable markers, and Polaroids of each family member, becomes a playful message centre and weekly planner. The set-up invites all family members to participate in scheduling (and impromptu artistry), which makes school runs, family dinners, and netball games easy to keep straight in a busy household.

display

The art of display is traditionally about showing our prized possessions to their greatest advantage. But there's also a subtler component: that of revealing the inner beauty in the everyday objects that fill our lives. A simple vase on an uncluttered shelf, a bowl filled with chestnuts from an autumn walk, a set of antique tools that relate to the work you love to do – all are made special when presented with authority. Whether you have a signed lithograph on hand to fill an empty wall or a collection of fifty-pence postcards, how you display things can

Judiciously displayed treasures can also help reinforce a sense of order in a workroom. Look for harmonious ways to group like objects or dissimilar ones. Unrelated photographs in colour and black and white can be identically framed to fill a wall to spectacular effect. With a box of drawing pins and a dozen album covers, you can create a themed gallery display. A collection of miniature cars might line a shelf, extending the length of a wall or encircling the room. A youth spent in football stands might be memorialized in a collage of ticket stubs arranged by date and

Display is not only the art of showing beautiful objects, but also of arranging ordinary ones so that their beauty – and the pleasure you take in them – becomes visible.

enliven a workroom's character and mood. From attic to pedestal, to honoured place on the shelf, display makes art of the special and ordinary objects that we pick up along the way.

In a workspace, the tools of your trade provide especially appealing material for display: stacks of books that reflect your professional passions, architectural drawings, city maps, photographs, or charcoal sketches. Even office supplies make a pleasing presentation when stored across a long shelf in colour-coded bins or neatly labelled binders. Anything that can be framed, hung, arranged on a mantel, or set on shelves can be turned into a compelling still-life display.

ground under a glass desktop. Group framed family photographs in clusters or in a long row where you'll be sure to see them.

When placing a display in a busy workroom that's already crowded with office supplies, try not to introduce too many separate collections. If you have an abundance of objects that you love, consider rotating them throughout the year to avoid cluttering your workspace. Allow each "exhibit" time to shine without competition, then simply rotate it out when you're ready for a new look. Chances are good that the change will trigger welcome inspiration in your work as well. Spending time with old friends usually does.

Lessons from a Painter's Studio

A working artist's studio uses the magic of colour and the power of shape to inspire creativity and define style. Painted bright white from floor to ceiling, the workspace doubles as an art gallery, turning even the most everyday objects into works of art on display.

The magic of colour – and the benefit of an entirely white palette – is in its ability to unify a busy workspace and serve competing needs for creativity and order. Few workrooms contain more tools – or guarantee more cleaning up – than an artist's studio. By "whiting out" the background with freshly painted walls, a room-size blank canvas is created and a new level of order – and possibility – becomes apparent.

In this painter's studio, attention is called not to clutter but to shape and colour. The striking, graphic wall display is beautiful in its own right, and it's a subtle reminder of the power of symmetry to free up the imagination. Graphic displays can be used to emphasize a room's theme, highlight its structure, or visually direct the gaze – and you don't have to be a certified artist to pull them off. Have a dozen of your favourite photographs blown up, mount them in frames, and arrange them in a grid. Experiment with different arrangements by first laying the frames on the floor, then hang your preferred combination. For a similar effect on a smaller scale, string rows of wire the length of a wall and hang your complete museum postcard collection. Even a series of mounted clips can create an artful display of your favourite maps, fabrics, or handmade wrapping paper.

A red carpenter's toolbox, *left*, stores supplies and holds its own against the vibrant wall display. **Flat file drawers for oversize drawings**, *right*, can be put to good use in any workspace for maps, photographs, large documents, or craft and gift-wrapping supplies.

In this busy studio, a generous work and storage area seems to float weightlessly in the centre of the room. Its position allows for easy traffic flow on all sides, and it is set low enough to permit clear sight lines across the room. A variety of displays – from a classic easel in the corner to improvised "easels" made of chairs, window ledges, and a shelf – allow art to dry while adding to the room's display.

A floating desktop, *above*, is made of a sheet of Perspex set on plumbing brackets. The resulting airspace permits tools and supplies to be neatly stored in full view, creating a mini display case when viewed from above. **The centre worktable**, *right*, includes generous storage and a work surface that can be accessed from all sides. The island's square shape echoes that of the wall display and its central position within the room.

Design Details

Artwork arranged in proportion to the space balances the room's symmetry.

An easel and a desk placed against a back wall create two discrete work zones.

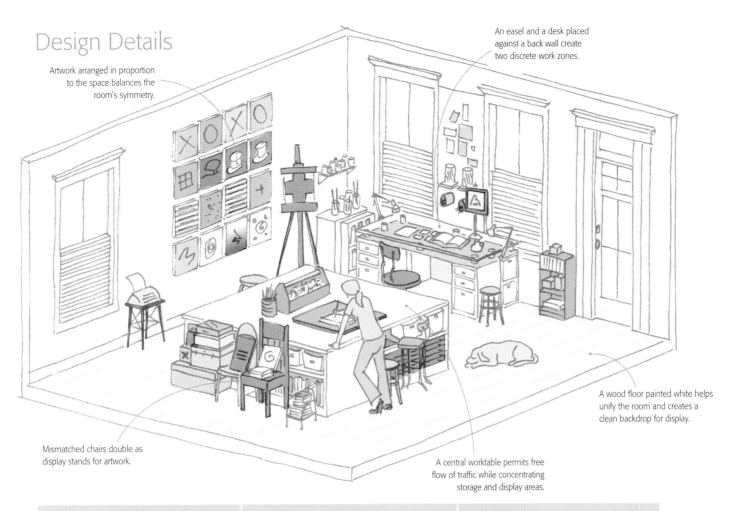

A wood floor painted white helps unify the room and creates a clean backdrop for display.

Mismatched chairs double as display stands for artwork.

A central worktable permits free flow of traffic while concentrating storage and display areas.

Colour Palette

Wall-to-wall and floor-to-ceiling white sets the stage in a studio bursting with colourful art. White can pull a workroom together, and serve as both blank canvas and organizing principle. In a crowded visual field, just as in a painting, red draws the eye first, helping the viewer to focus and enter into the environment. Black accents offer a point of reflection and repose, and are an excellent anchoring point in a large space.

Room Plan

A massive work island in the centre of this artist's studio defines the space architecturally, while freeing up walls for display and an alternative desk area. Locating the principal workspace in the middle of the room also reduces clutter and improves traffic flow. The island's grand dimensions make it possible to leave both supplies and works-in-progress out as needed. A separate work area positioned against the wall for smaller projects or routine office duties helps keep order in a room filled with creative inspiration.

Materials

Painted floors Hardwood floors coated with a durable paint formula (some are made especially for floors) can unify a workroom.

Perspex An acrylic material valued for its toughness and close resemblance to glass, Perspex is lighter than glass.

Canvas Washable cotton canvas works as well for office storage bins as it does for loose covers. Look for bins in heavyweight fabrics, so they'll hold their shape.

Small Space Workplace

A reverence for beautiful tools and an instinct for order combine to turn a small artist's studio into a functional work of art. Spare furnishings and neat stacks allow the items on display to inspire.

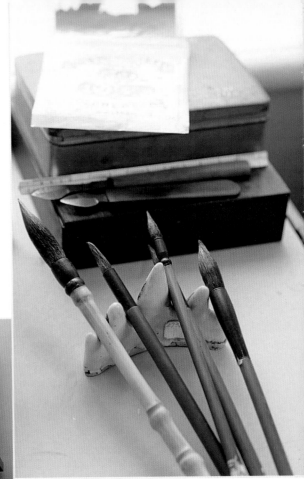

Creating a beautiful workroom need not depend on expensive furnishings or lots of space. This artist's enclave (inspired by Chinese scholars' studios) shows that you can arrange everyday objects and hand tools to compose a workspace as you would a picture. Here, every element rewards the eye with beauty, from the slender wooden ladder propped against the wall as a display stand and drying rack to the stepped towers of oversize art books that rise from the floor.

A small-scale secretaire, *left*, stores and displays artists' tools. **A display of calligraphy pens**, *above*, emphasizes the craft. **Transparent pages of lettering**, *right*, take advantage of the sunlight.

A Home Office Gallery

Bold displays of family photographs and memorabilia on office walls and shelves are like scrapbooks writ large. Mix old and new photographs with maps and mementos to make a gallery-style exhibit of your family's happiest memories, achievements, and rites of passage.

Assembling a display of family photographs and mementos is one of life's more rewarding pastimes. Afternoons spent sifting through boxes of old letters and ticket stubs, sorting and framing photos of old friends and interesting ancestors, are repaid by the delight of reacquaintance. Turning those efforts into an office gallery display ensures that the pleasure is an ongoing one, and can make your workspace intriguing to family and visitors alike.

Surrounding yourself with familiar faces as you work provides both inspiration and comfort. Executed with the kind of panache on view in this home office, a gallery-style display gives a room architectural definition and emotional power. You can adapt photo arrangements to just about any style of shelving or wall space. Whether you display your treasures on a bare wall, under glass, or on a few modest shelves, do it with curatorial confidence. Mix frame sizes and shapes. For a museum-quality display, allow room for experimentation, as this office does, and dedicate a pinboard to experiments, giving pride of place to finished pieces.

A crisscross of rope between shelves, *left*, adds the casual element of a pinboard to a more formal gallery display. Clipped snapshots can be rotated as desired. **A collection of family photographs**, *right*, links several generations. Framed photos on top are part of the "permanent collection".

This capacious workroom is just the spot for a prominent display. Here, narrow black shelves are an orderly way to display a large art collection. Shelves and ledges also allow you to move framed pictures around easily, without making a lot of nail holes. In this shared office, an assortment of family photos is made contemporary with simple new frames.

A changing gallery of mementos celebrates a family's travels and illustrates its history.

To frame like an expert, choose mounts that are acid-neutral (the acid in some paper stock can cause photos to deteriorate) and make sure that the opening in the mount is slightly smaller than the photo. To prevent photos from buckling, attach them only to the top of the mount before framing. Irreplaceable photographs should be copied; frame one set and keep the originals in archival boxes for safekeeping and easy retrieval.

Protective plastic boxes on the coffee table, *left*, make it easy to examine valuable family documents up close; property deeds and army records help to locate family members in time and place. **A built-in light box**, *right*, allows for easy identification of old negatives.

A sense of scale and proportion is essential to an attractive display. Organizing pictures and other materials by date or theme gives coherence to a large collection.

Albums don't do favourite photos justice: get them out of the scrapbook and into the office so you can enjoy them every day.

The spirit of your family might best be conveyed through a multi-generational sports portfolio, a series of personal memoirs, a display of regional folk art, or a collection of handwritten recipes. Academic or artistic achievements, birth certificates, marriage licences, and naturalization papers are all eminently worth framing. Combining such documents with photos of the people whose names appear on them is a way to honour the past and its meaning to the life you live today.

A desk-blotter photo collage, *left*, and an articulated desk lamp brighten an ebonized work surface. **A corkboard map of the United States**, *right*, traces emmigrant ancestors from landings in Boston and Pennsylvania to a chance meeting on a Colorado ski slope.

Design Details

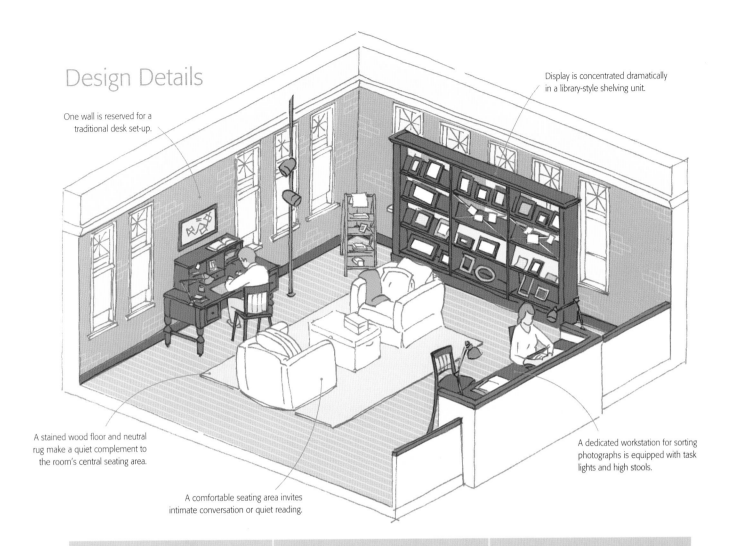

Display is concentrated dramatically in a library-style shelving unit.

One wall is reserved for a traditional desk set-up.

A stained wood floor and neutral rug make a quiet complement to the room's central seating area.

A comfortable seating area invites intimate conversation or quiet reading.

A dedicated workstation for sorting photographs is equipped with task lights and high stools.

Colour Palette

The soft, mottled pink of aged terracotta brickwork has a beauty and authority that few painted-on colours can match. It calls for a restrained hand and clean and simple colours, such as the classic black and white judiciously employed for trim and furniture in this spacious office. The glossy black of the desks and display case add drama and sophistication, as the white of the seating area defines an oasis for relaxing.

Room Plan

The multiple uses of this family home office and gallery are served well by a careful subdivision of the space into four discrete zones. Desks positioned on opposite sides of the room permit two or more people to work in relative privacy at the same time. A seating area in the centre of the room gives the large space both a visual focus and a welcome spot for conversation or reading, while leaving an entire wall free for a museum-style display. The open shelving of the display walls highlights the purpose of this project room with a photographic family history.

Materials

Brick Rectangular blocks of natural clay baked in a kiln or direct sun until hard, bricks have been used in all types of construction for millennia.

Twill A tightly woven textured fabric identified by its diagonal grain, twill is durable, versatile, and gets softer with each washing.

Wool A traditional fibre for carpets and rugs, wool is long lasting, soil resistant, and an effective insulator. It adds texture to a room.

How to Personalize a Bulletin Board

Every workspace needs a place to put invitations, business cards, photos, tickets, and important notes. It's obvious that these reminders should be easy to see, so why not turn the especially nice ones into an artful display? Take a lesson from primary school and create a bulletin board, but instead of posting stars for yourself, transform your important bits of paper into a distinctive arrangement. Unlikely household goods sometimes make the most attractive options: metal signs fitted with magnetic clips, hanging lengths of bungee cords with notes pinned into them, or shadow boxes displaying business cards and mementos.

A metal U rescued from an old sign, *above*, has been transformed into a graphic notice board that would look equally at home in a study, project room, or hallway. Prop it on a shelf or mount it on a wall, provide plenty of magnetic clips, and watch it fill up. **A useful update of the velvet painting**, *right*, turns an elegant gilded frame into a unique pinboard. A standard corkboard covered in richly coloured burgundy velvet is framed as lovingly as a prized painting to elevate everyday notes, sketches, and reminders to the level of high art.

An old-fashioned pinboard, *left*, and a retro-style telephone to go with it, are just the things for those who work best with everything all in one place, from business cards to recipes. **An empty frame**, *below*, fitted with a sheet of tempered glass, turns any wall in the house into a memorable message centre. Jot down messages and phone numbers directly on the glass in any colour you wish (remember to use erasable markers or wax pencils). Post invitations, postcards, and concert or sports tickets with tape for easy removal without leaving a trace.

How to Display Collections

A display should capture your attention as soon as you walk into a room. Whether you have museum-quality artwork to hang, tin musical instruments to show off, or vintage postcards to line up on a shelf, every collection makes its own demands for space, light, and the right setting. A display can be a formal presentation or an offhand column of oversized books doubling as a side table, but all displays should offer a sense of discovery. To create an intimate atmosphere and invite a closer look at a favourite collection, display pieces where they can be seen up close and handled.

Small-scale architectural models, *above*, are set on top of pillars as proud examples of the architect's craft. Show off the rewards of hard work by displaying your presentations, artwork, or manuscripts, whether in progress or completed.
A row of favourite books, *right*, is held in place by a miniature wooden chair and a typesetter's frame.

A clean-lined wooden chair, *left*, serves as an easel for books and artwork. Displays of collections are especially effective when they combine the practical with the treasured in surprising compositions. **A shelf of music**, *below*, is set off by a 1940s microphone; a miniature Vespa scooter claims centre stage on a display centred around a retro music theme.

Room Resources

Casual style is something you can weave through every space in your home, from front rooms to private havens. For this book, we scoured hundreds of locations to find perfect settings to create rooms just for you. We experimented with colours, lighting, furnishings, rugs, curtains, and accessories to find the best combinations for each space. The results? This collection of style ideas, which we hope will inspire and delight you.

Each location chosen for this book was unique and interesting. Here is a little bit more about each of the homes we visited, the style ideas we created, and the individual elements that make each design tick.

A note about colour: wherever it was possible in this list of resources, we've offered the actual paint manufacturer and paint colour that was used in the room shown. We also list the closest Benjamin Moore paint colour match (in parentheses). Because photography and colour printing processes can dramatically change the way colours appear, it is very important to test swatches of any paint colour you are considering in your own home, where you can see how the light affects them at different times of the day.

At Home in the Office

Under the eaves of a classic Victorian townhouse, this second-storey office with dormer windows overlooks a busy city street.

Space This high-ceilinged office shares the top storey with the master bedroom. Walls, ceilings, and trim are all painted in the same tint of white to reflect light and minimize the shadows created by the eaves. Floors are narrow-board oak.

Colour Walls (Benjamin Moore Snowfall White OC-118, flat).

Furnishings Grayson leather chair, Sutton bookcase, Classic Grand phone, Bedford filing boxes and stand, linen solid sisal rug, Dashboard clock, Sailcloth curtain, and Eclipse rod, all from Pottery Barn. Coffee table painted with blackboard paint from Benjamin Moore. Linen button-tufted love seat, Sony Vaio computer, vintage oak desk, vintage milking stool, and Bose Wave radio.

Lighting Wrought iron floor lamp with grass-cloth drum shade, and a pair of wooden table lamps, all circa 1950. PB basic lampshades from Pottery Barn.

pages 14–19

Working with an Open-Plan Scheme

The home office of an architect, this spacious loft is on the top storey of a stucco house built in 1912.

Space The office occupies a storey and features exposed ceiling structure with floating platforms for recessed cove lighting. The dramatic stairwell is a feature that divides the expansive space, and is illuminated by a skylight.

Colour Walls (Benjamin Moore White Chocolate OC-127).

Furnishings Malabar Chair, weathered wooden tables, Folsom collection leather desktop accessories, Bedford files, and twill cushions, all from Pottery Barn. Aeron desk chairs by Herman Miller. Home design series personal audio system CD player by Sony. Power Mac G4 computer and cinema display by Apple Computer. Designer series trolley by All Crate. Custom-made Perspex desktops.

Lighting Recessed halogen lights in ceiling, brushed steel incandescent Architect desk lamps by Tensor.

Display Architecture scale models: pages 27 and 29 by Naylor & Chu; pages 24, 25, and 27 by BRU Architects; large white model on stairwell by John Owen.

pages 24–31

A Working Guest Room

A guest bedroom tucked in the refurbished attic of this 1930s stuccoed home also serves as a writer's home office.

Space In this diminutive bedroom, an all-white palette reflects light and makes the small space seem larger. The desk and truckle bed create a continuous line that unifies the room's far wall.

Colour Walls (Benjamin Moore Old Prairie 2143-50).

Furnishings Thomas day-bed, shadow box frames, abaca rug, Retro radio, suede patchwork cushions, and Classic Grand phone, all from Pottery Barn. Desk chair by Lounge, San Francisco. Vintage typewriters (left to right): Underwood, Argyle P201, Remington Portable, and Remington Travel-Riter.

Lighting Swing arm lamps from Ikea.

Display 1940s and '50s novels courtesy of Helfond Books, San Anselmo, CA.

pages 32–37

Putting Colour to Work

A graceful Victorian house overlooking a city park, this 12-room residence was built in 1891 and was occupied by the same family for fifty years.

Space Although the room is only 2.7 x 3 m (9 x 10 ft), it has 3.5 m (12 ft) ceilings and oversize windows with large, decorative carved mouldings – hallmarks of its Victorian-era architecture.

Colour Walls Full spectrum Phillips Perfect Colors paint (Benjamin Moore Straw 2154-50).

Furnishings Ariana leather chair, classic twill striped cushion, Sundari kilim, studio wall shelf, Schoolhouse side chair, Folsom collection leather bags and blotter, and ash poster frame, all from Pottery Barn. Zinc desk from Swallowtail, San Francisco. Vintage ladder from Zonal, San Francisco. Antique boxes from Luck Would Have It, Mill Valley, CA.

Lighting Cortland kitchen brass pendant fixture and Haley lamp with linen shade, all from Pottery Barn.

pages 46–51

Planning a Garden Workroom

The outbuildings dotting this property are reminiscent of old Hawaiian plantation sheds.

Space Sharing the grounds with two other outbuildings, this potting shed is set behind a Craftsman bungalow and is adjacent to a large garden.

Furnishings Garden umbrella, galvanized bar container, galvanized ice bucket, Everlife clock, Augusta wicker chair, bushel baskets, and Daily wall system, all from Pottery Barn. Green watering can and Conservatory can by Smith & Hawken. White plaster topiary, white enamelware flower buckets, glass garden cloche, appertif glasses, ceramic cheese dome, hessian-covered pinboard, laboratory vessel, Vermont sap buckets, and anti-fatigue runner. Vintage mercury glass gazing ball.

Lighting Vintage camp lantern.

Display Vintage greengrocer signs from Portobello Market, London. Vintage padlock and horseshoe collections.

pages 58–65

Basics of a Welcoming Workspace

This 1884 building was built as the gardener's quarters on an estate that was refurbished in 1998.

Space Twin rooms flanking a hallway, this working home-office suite features custom wooden blinds. The fir floors extend throughout the house.

Colour Walls (Benjamin Moore Celadon Green 2028-60).

Furnishings Westport seating in sage twill, shadow box frames, and Lewis storage cube, all from Pottery Barn. Aeron desk chair by Herman Miller. Brancusi-inspired plinths, and ladder bookshelves originally designed for retail displays. Contemporary plywood chair. Kosta Boda tall white vase and ceramic vessel, both from Verdi, San Francisco. Hand-blown glass bottles from Poland.

Lighting Gallery lights from Pottery Barn. Clip-on light from Target.

Display Easel from Flax Art & Design, San Francisco. Magnetic whiteboard from Ikea. Vintage botany posters from Clignancourt Flea Market, France. Frames from Painter's Place, San Francisco.

pages 72–79

Serene Style for a Bedroom Study

This recently renovated cottage has large, custom-designed windows to take advantage of a hillside view.

Space During the renovation by architect Andrew Mann, the grey paint colour on the trim in the window alcove was specially chosen to reflect the changing patterns of shadows in the bedroom as the sun moves throughout the day.

Colour Walls (Benjamin Moore White Diamond 2121-60). Arch trim (Benjamin Moore Gray Cashmere 2138-60).

Furnishings Hayley bench and dining table, Megan office chair, draughtboard rug, Sausalito Roman blinds, leather lumbar cushions, PB Basic Hemstitch bedding, silk and velvet quilt, wire leaf basket, and wicker baskets, all from Pottery Barn. Sony Vaio computer. Amber resin boxes by Martha Sturdy, Vancouver, Canada.

Lighting Glass lamp from Pottery Barn.

Display Artwork (from left to right): Leaf Study #1, 2002; Leaf Study #7, 2003; Leaf Study #2, 2002; all by Thomas Hayes courtesy of Sears-Peyton Gallery, New York City.

pages 82–87

The Right Light, Day or Night

This combination pool house–office is on a hillside estate that overlooks vineyards.

Space The traditional farm buildings found on old winery estates inspired the exposed structure of the office.

Colour Walls (Benjamin Moore White Heron OC-57).

Furnishings Megan chairs loose-covered in twill, canvas utility bags, colour bound sisal rug, Cabot coffee table, Batik cushion, Veranda stripe cushions, and chenille throw, all from Pottery Barn. Canvas sorting bin by Todd Oldham for Target. Sony Computer model SDM 981. Canvas contractor's bags by Klein Tools.

Lighting Gallery sconces and touch lamp from Pottery Barn. Billy lights from Ikea.

Display Vintage Pottery Barn Jonathan Adler vessels. Vintage Staffordshire blue striped bowls, vintage French flash cards, and enamel funnels circa 1920 from Yankee Girl, San Anselmo, CA.

pages 96–103

Outfitting a Workshop

The design of this woodworker's office employs boat-construction techniques the homeowner learned from his shipbuilder father.

Space The 22 sq m (240 sq ft) office is built primarily of mill fall down (wood left over after the milling process). The floor is white oak, and the trim is redwood.

Colour Pegboard (Benjamin Moore Hamilton Blue, Ext. Rm).

Furnishings Savannah baskets, Bedford hutch, and Schoolhouse desk chair, all from Pottery Barn. Industrial anti-fatigue matting from Home Depot. Antique drawing board stool from Yankee Girl, San Anselmo, CA.

Lighting Parisian task lamp from Pottery Barn. Clip-on desk lamp.

Display Collection of antique woodworking tools courtesy of John Owen. Wooden trays custom built in teak, Douglas fir, and cherry by Arch Design, San Rafael, CA. Turned wooden items above window frame: Brancusi-inspired toy plinth, turned cylinder in soft pine, antique wooden plane, and rosewood bowl.

pages 112–119

Options for an Organized Office

The homeowners designed this modern structure with garage-style glass doors to open onto a hillside.

Space The office loft is 5.8 m (19 ft) long and contains a sliding bookshelf wall that separates master bedroom from work space. The 2.2 m- (7 ft-) long desk was custom-built for the space.

Colour Walls (Benjamin Moore Powder Sand 2151-70).

Furnishings Burton studio sofa, Grayson leather chair, Savannah basket, Gabbeh rug, drinks trolley, and leather cushions, all from Pottery Barn. Custom-fit magnetic memo boards in shelves.

Lighting Jean-Paul floor lamp and table lamp from Pottery Barn.

Display Wall easel from Pottery Barn. Black-and-white photo in wall easel by Darryl Estrine.

pages 128–135

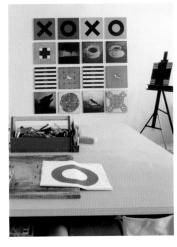

A Working Holiday

Surrounded by rose gardens and tall hedges, the front portion of this clapboard house was built in 1856, with an extension built in 1930.

Space The 5.5 x 2.7 m (18 x 9 ft) office is a first-storey sleeping veranda that was converted and enclosed during the 1930s. It connects to the rest of house through the master bedroom.

Colour Walls (Benjamin Moore Nantucket Fog AC-22, semi gloss). Trim (Benjamin Moore Chantilly Lace, OC-65).

Furnishings Fringed jute rug, Augusta wicker chair, Farmhouse benches and occasional table, Estate pewter tray, Savannah baskets, and linen cushion, all from Pottery Barn. Vintage ticking-stripe towel from Williams-Sonoma. Circa 1920s painted occasional table. Vintage clock face, Pyrex cloches, vintage painted cutlery tray, vintage dish drainer, pewter and silver baby cups and loving cups, porcelain tap fittings used as key chains, Violet ink box holds stamps. Attic vents hold letters.

Lighting Claro lamp from Pottery Barn.

Display Starfish are labelled with names of the beaches where they were found.

pages 144–51

Lessons from a Painter's Studio

This cottage was converted to a studio by its artist owner. The rear opens to a small garden courtyard.

Space Beam structure is left exposed to add height to the room, and clip-on lights are used to keep wiring to a minimum.

Colour Walls (Benjamin Moore Sebring White, OC-137).

Furnishings Schoolhouse chair, Bedford modular filing system, canvas utility bags, and modern shelves, all from Pottery Barn. Custom-designed Perspex desk. Vintage painted and stencilled chair. Vintage carpenter's toolbox, wooden flat filing drawers, and trunk collection.

Lighting Hardware store clamp lights

Display 40 x 40 cm (16 x 16 in) oil-on-canvas paintings by Joyce Robertson, www.joycerobertson.com.

pages 162–167

A Home Office Gallery

Built in 1911 with a Carnegie grant, this building was once the town's library and was converted to a residence in the early 1970s.

Space The lofty two-level house is 427 sq m (4,600 sq ft), with Douglas fir floors and original windows detailed with the cross of St. Andrew at the top.

Colour Window sills and built-in shelves (Benjamin Moore Cream Silk, OC-115). Ceiling (Benjamin Moore Simply White, OC-117). Worktop, shelving unit, and skirting boards (Benjamin Moore Universal Black, 2118-10, high gloss).

Furnishings Gustavian bar stools, Charleston square chairs, gallery frames, Aris desk with chest, Gustavian chair, Sutton bookcases, cork map board, Heathered self-bound sisal rug, and gallery frames, all from Pottery Barn. Original library shelving. Vintage steamer trunk used as occasional table.

Lighting Flood lights and autopole provided by Da Vinci Fusion, San Francisco. Halogen track lighting.

Display Vintage photo collection and vintage collector's cupboard.

pages 170–177

Glossary

Abaca An exceptionally strong fibre, abaca comes from the leafstalk of a banana plant native to the Philippines, where it's been cultivated since the sixteenth century. Abaca becomes a comfortable and durable natural textile when woven into twine, rugs, or fabric.

Adirondack chair During the late nineteenth century, the Adirondack Park holiday area in the northeast US state of New York became the inspiration for a style of handcrafted outdoor furniture that used rough planks from a hemlock tree.

Aeron chair Produced by Herman Miller, a manufacturer known for both its contemporary office furniture and modern classics, the Aeron chair was designed in 1994 by Don Chadwick and Bill Stumpf. Lauded as an innovative breakthrough in office-chair design, the Aeron is lightweight and ergonomic.

Anti-fatigue matting Used primarily in industrial work environments, anti-fatigue matting offers a cushioned surface that eases standing for long periods of time. Usually made of rubber, these mats are meant to be slip-resistant and durable.

Anodized aluminium Treated with an electrolytic process to create a protective coating, anodized aluminium is easier to produce than steel though equally sturdy. In the mid-twentieth century, mass-produced metal office furnishings were commonly made of this material.

Architectural salvage Recovered or antique parts of a building, including decorative mouldings, columns, millwork, corbels, cornices, and window sashes, architectural salvage has become a collectable accessory that adds a fanciful and unique touch to a room's decor.

Articulated lamps This type of task lighting, particularly swivel, stork-style, or swing-arm lamps that have working hinges, allow the fixture to be adjusted and the light focussed in any direction.

Blackboard paint This topcoat speciality paint allows you to transform furniture, walls, and floors into blackboards. For best results, the surface should be smooth; unpainted surfaces require a coat of primer before application.

Built-in storage Fabricated specifically for a particular space, built-in storage, whether cabinetry or shelving, is designed to be part of a room's architecture. By fitting precisely into a wall, built-in storage takes up less floor space than free-standing storage.

Canvas Made from linen or cotton, this heavy-duty fabric is commonly used for sporting goods, awnings, and outdoor furnishings. When used for storage bins, curtains, loose covers, or cushions, it adds a casual and relaxed feel to a room.

Cast iron Sometimes confused with wrought iron, cast iron is made by pouring molten iron into a mould to create a decorative or practical shape.

Chicken wire This light-gauge wire mesh has a hexagonal pattern and is often used as fencing. For a French country look, replace the glass in cupboard door frames with chicken wire.

Chrome A hard metallic element that takes a high polish, chrome plating is used in furnishings to prevent corrosion. When brushed, the usually reflective finish is dulled and the surface gains a smooth, silver sheen.

Dormer window This type of window is set vertically into a small gable projecting from a sloping roof; the gable holding such a window is often called a dormer.

Eaves The overhang of a roof beyond the facade of a building. Inside the house, slanted space beneath the eaves is often a good place to install storage.

Enamelware Metal dishware coated in thin layers of enamel – a smooth, glassy glaze. Enamelware is well suited for use outdoors or in humid areas such as a greenhouse because it is rustproof.

Ergonomics Also referred to as "human engineering", ergonomics focusses on the design and application of objects for safe and efficient interaction with people. Office ergonomics are generally focussed on the health, comfort, and safety of workers at their desks.

Flat file drawers Wide, shallow drawers, in cabinets are ideal for storing large-scale items such as blueprints, maps, handmade paper, or artwork.

Gallery lights So-called because galleries and museums employ these lights to illuminate artwork, gallery lights use adjustable, low-level halogen bulbs that direct light onto hanging art or any object mounted on the wall.

Galvanized metal Metal is galvanized by coating it with a thin layer of another metal (usually zinc) to form a protective finish. The distinctive mottled look of galvanized metal adds a raw, industrial feel to indoor and outdoor furnishings.

Graduated storage Containers or shelves of varying sizes that are stacked or lined up from smallest to largest, often to make the most of a tight space.

Halogen A modern refinement of the incandescent light bulb, these lamps are filled with halogen gas and offer bright, white light, compact size, energy efficiency, and a longer lifespan than incandescent bulbs. Halogen casts a light tone that reads truer to natural light than incandescent or fluorescent bulbs.

Hessian A loosely woven, coarse fabric made of jute fibres, hessian is often used for agricultural or horticultural purposes. The natural, rustic appearance of hessian adds a comforting earthiness to a room's decor.

Kilims These reversible flat-weave wool rugs originated with the nomadic peoples of Iran, Iraq, Pakistan, and Turkey. Designed to be placed on sandy desert floors, they feature bold, intricate motifs, each one representing a different tribe or region.

Linen Woven from the fibres of the flax plant, linen can be as fine and sheer as a handkerchief or as substantial as a canvas. Twice as strong as cotton, linen softens with each washing. This versatile fabric is commonly used for loose covers or upholstery. Lightweight linen curtains offer privacy while allowing diffuse sunlight to shine through.

Mahogany This fine-grained hardwood varies in colour from golden brown to deep red brown and is used for the manufacture of cabinetry, panelling, interior trim, doors, decorative borders, fine furniture, and even flooring.

Marble Used for interior surfaces such as walls, furniture, and worktops, polished marble has a glossy surface that reflects light and emphasizes this beautiful stone's colour and markings.

Milk glass Named for its signature opaque white colouring, milk glass can also be found in colours such as blue or pink. These highly collectable pieces are often intricately detailed and produced from moulds; covered dishes featuring animal motifs are particularly popular.

Milk paint A mix of casein (powdered milk protein), lime, and stable earth pigments, milk paint was a popular interior finish during the Colonial era in the United States. Environmentally friendly, this paint dries quickly to a hard, flat finish that can be sanded, distressed, oiled, waxed, polished, or varnished.

Mohair The hair of Angora goats, mohair is characterized by a smooth, silky feel. It is spun into yarn, which is then woven into fabric. The term mohair can refer to the yarn, the fabric, or an imitation.

Mouldings This architectural term most commonly refers to the decorative strip of carved wood that finishes doorways, windows, chair rails, ceilings, and walls.

Open plan An open-plan room is designed with few walls or architectural obstructions to create one large, lofty space. In a workroom, the open-plan approach allows creativity with furniture placement; desks can be set in the centre of a room for 360-degree access.

Panelling Originally developed to prevent wall damage in heavy-traffic areas, panelling usually refers to wooden boards that cover the lower portion of a wall. The term can also refer to full-height wall panelling. Beadboard, which has a regular raised pattern on the wood, is a common type of panelling.

Patina When the effects of age and use transform the surface of a material, this is often referred to as a patina. A classic example is the green layer that forms on copper or bronze over time, when it's exposed to outdoor elements.

Pegboard Fibreboard building material with evenly spaced holes for holding hooks, shelves, or pegs. Tools or other items hung from the hooks or stacked between pegs remain easily visible and accessible. Pegboard can be found in sleek, metal versions as well.

Perspex This trademarked name refers to clear acrylic sheets that are used as protective barriers in much the same way that glass is used. Covering a table or desk, Perspex protects the surface and creates a display area under the acrylic.

Pinboard A board used for posting notices, reminders, inspirations, and other items. Like a bulletin board, a pinboard can be fashioned from any material onto which notes can be affixed.

Pine One of the most common soft-woods, pine comes from a coniferous tree (which produces cones), making it softer than hardwoods from deciduous trees (which shed leaves). Still, it's a popular choice for furnishings and flooring because of its rustic, knotty grain.

Redwood While any wood that produces a red dye is considered a redwood, the most famous are the California coast redwoods, which grow up to 110 m (360 ft) in height. This durable hardwood is used in both interiors and exteriors, including architectural detailing, panelling, decking, and rustic furniture.

Roll-top desk This type of writing desk can be closed by rolling down a cover, which is usually made from thin strips of wood attached to a flexible backing.

Roman blinds Drawn up from the bottom by means of cords and rings, these blinds create horizontal folds when raised. A Roman blind panel is flat when lowered and usually covers the entire window glass completely.

Sawhorse desk A simple desk made by laying a board over two sawhorses, which are A-shaped frames originally intended to support wood for sawing.

Secretaire A compact desk with a top section for books and a writing surface that closes up to present a smooth, uncluttered front, secretaires originated in Europe as portable writing desks during the seventeenth century.

Shadow box A shallow, closed-frame box that allows you to display and protect three-dimensional artwork, books, or mementos behind glass.

Sisal This flexible fibre is made from the leaves of the sisal (or agave) plant, which grows in Africa and South America. Softer to the touch than jute, but still durable, sisal is commonly woven into flat rugs with an even, highly textural surface. Sisal rugs hide dirt, resist stains, and absorb sounds, making them practical for high-traffic areas.

Ticking Originally used to make mattress and pillow coverings, this strong, tightly woven cotton fabric features a signature pattern of simple stripes against a natural background.

Twill This smooth, durable fabric is tightly woven, usually of cotton, and has a raised diagonal weave. A good choice for loose covers or upholstery, denim and gabardine are examples of twill. Brushed twill is finished to emphasize the fabric's soft nap.

Vintage suitcases Pieces of luggage intended to be carried comfortably by hand, suitcases can also work as discreet storage when stacked as a side table or filing tower.

Vellum A parchment paper traditionally made of calfskin, lambskin, or kidskin, vellum was once used as a writing material. Modern vellum is made from plant fibres and is prized for its smoothness and transparency, making it a good choice for lampshades.

Wax pencils Used to mark smooth surfaces such as glass, Perspex, or metal, these pencils (also called Chinagraph pencils) are particularly useful for jotting down temporary notes, because the marks can easily be wiped away.

Wicker Created by weaving flexible lengths of plants such as bamboo, cane, rattan, reed, or willow around a sturdy frame, wicker is commonly used to make baskets and furniture. A durable material, wicker can stand up to a century of normal use.

Wrought iron This commercial grade of iron is bent into shape to create decorative and durable architectural elements such as grates, balconies, fences, and stair railings. Decorative styles include Gothic tracery, plant forms, and classical motifs. Today, wrought iron is sometimes actually made of steel.

Zinc This crystalline metallic element has an initial sheen that is similar to stainless steel's, but zinc weathers to a matt, blue-grey patina over time. Prized for its softly worn finish, zinc is often used as a protective coating for iron or steel – a process that results in galvanized metal.

Zoning Dividing a room or space into zones or sections reserved for different purposes can be accomplished with the help of furnishings, lighting, or accessories. For example, a home office might have different zones for reading, filing, and computer work.

Index